Collins Revised

Engaging English 4

Ruby Bose

Components of DigiSuite

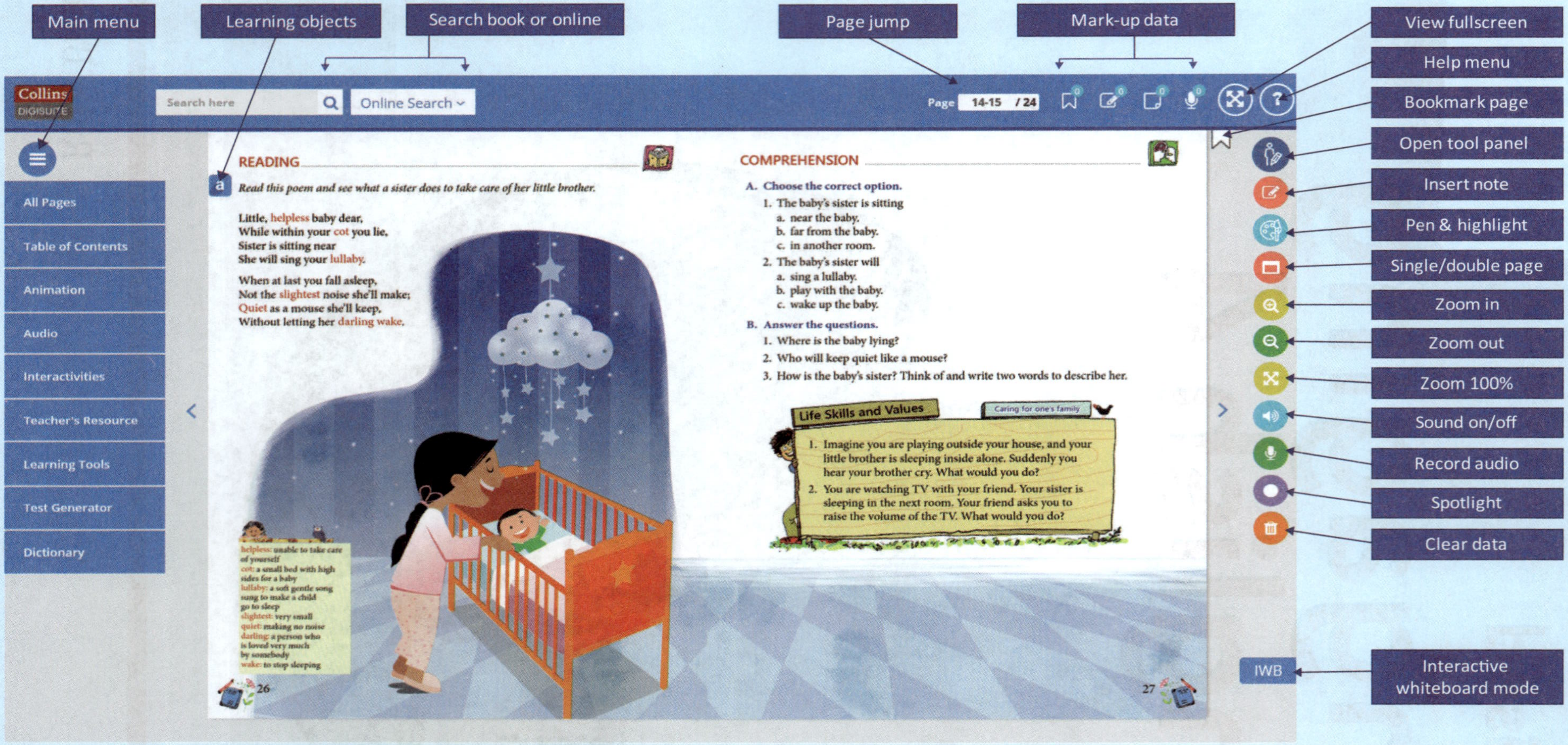

Student + Teacher

- a — animations
- ilt — instructor-led tutorials
- ia — activities
- w — worksheets
- audio
- g — games
- v — videos

Teacher-only

- lp — lesson plans
- w — worksheets
- tn — teacher's notes
- ak — answer keys

Preface

Revised Engaging English aims to instill an appreciation for literature in today's learners, while equipping them with the tools to develop native fluency and communicative competence in using the English language.

This eight-level series has been designed to teach language skills through the use of literature. Comprising Coursebooks and Workbooks, and digital resources for teachers for all levels, the series is meant to be educative as well as inspiring, imparting moral values and arousing the learner's curiosity about the world beyond the classroom.

In the revised edition, the series has been aligned closely with the guidelines of the National Education Policy, 2020 through its focus on twenty-first century skills, Sustainable Development Goals (SDGs), cross-curricular learning, 'Happiness' content and art-integrated learning. Coursebooks 1 and 2 integrate the essence of NIPUN (National Initiative for Proficiency in Reading with Understanding and Numeracy), which deals with Foundational Literacy and Numeracy. They aim to motivate students to read independently, improve their vocabulary, develop their critical thinking and creative skills and enhance their ability to express themselves verbally and in writing.

The lessons are built around carefully selected literary pieces with distinct cross-curricular themes, and presented with glossary, explanation of literary terms and interesting trivia. The end-of-chapter exercises address the needs of formal language learning and cover all aspects of language acquisition. They include *Comprehension, Way with Words, Grammar in Use, Study Skills, Listening and Speaking* and *Pen it Down*.

New Features in the Revised Edition

Let's Get Started: A theme-based, cross-curricular warm-up task at the beginning of each lesson spanning subjects like science, history and general knowledge, with a focus on SDGs.

Graphic stories: These include both fiction and non-fiction and address the needs of visual learners.

Cross-curricular trivia: This includes **Did You Know?**, which has interesting information covering science, mathematics, geography, history and general knowledge, related to the passage.

In-text questions: These assess while-reading comprehension of the learner.

Life Skills and Values: A part of Comprehension, this includes questions that encourage learners to think analytically and write creatively, thus building higher order thinking skills. They are aligned to the twenty-first century skills.

Augmented scaffolding: This comprises more detailed explanations for every section, including Way with Words and Grammar in Use. Concepts are presented through graphic organizers and reinforced through practice and repetition. Support is provided for the Listening and Speaking and Pen it Down tasks in the form of suggested points as well as useful words and phrases to facilitate competency-based learning.

Now I can: This is a learner-centric self-assessment checklist of the learning objectives for every lesson.

Be Creative!/Research and Write: These special pages, of which there are three in each book, include several new research-based literary projects, creative writing and vocabulary tasks which revisit the themes of the lessons. These focus variously on art integration and SDGs and support inquiry-based learning.

The **Workbooks** complement the Coursebooks by providing additional skills practice through the careful mapping of grammar and vocabulary. Each Workbook from Classes 3 to 8 includes a test paper based on the principle of SAFAL (Structured Assessment For Analyzing Learning), a competency-based assessment introduced by CBSE in keeping with the guidelines of the NEP. They focus on assessing the competencies of critical thinking as well as inquiry-based and analysis-based learning.

The series is supported with **Teacher's Resource Books** and **Digital resources**.

The series encourages competency-based education which allows concept acquisition at the learner's own pace, based on individual ability. We hope that it will foster a love for literature and reading in young learners.

Author

Ruby Bose has been teaching English for more than a decade at The Heritage School, Kolkata.

Key Features

Let's Get Started

- Theme-based warm-up activities, with a focus on Sustainable Development Goals

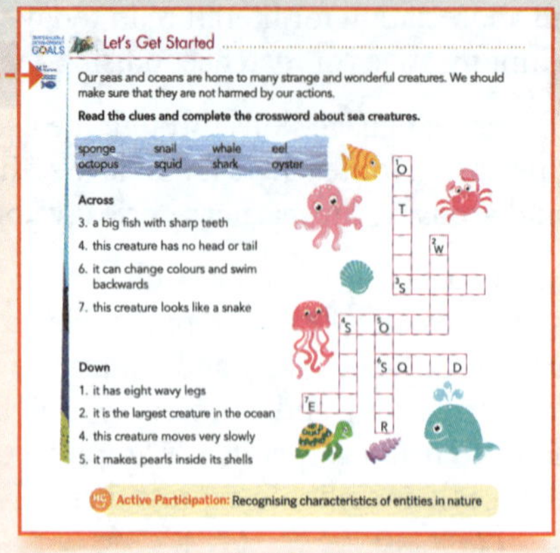

Reading

- Has a rich variety of reading passages, including prose, poetry and drama
- Covers literary genres like short stories, biographies, folktales, fables, fantasy, science fiction, non-fiction, extracts from contemporary and classic works, taken from Indian and world literature

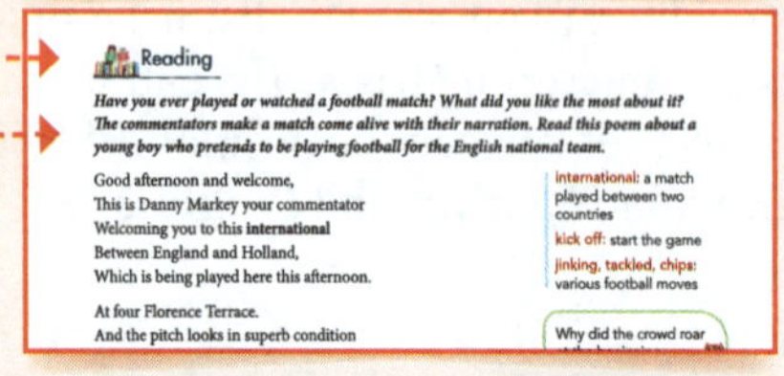

Introduction

- Includes background information about the reading text to initiate learners into the passage

Wordwise

- Provides additional information on the origin of words to interest learners in the nuances of language and to improve vocabulary

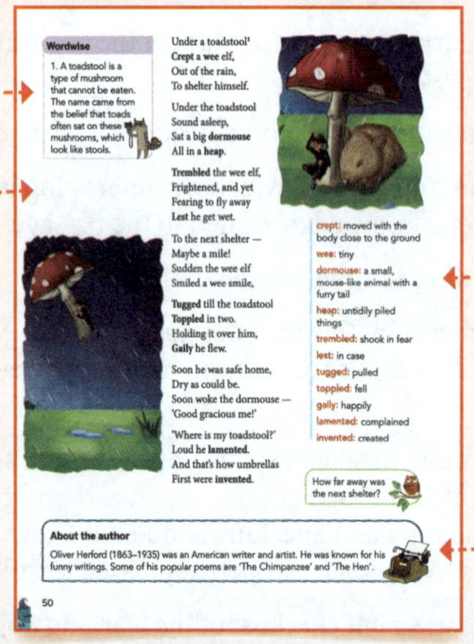

In-text questions

- 'while-reading' questions to check textual understanding

Comprehension

- 'Quick Recap' checks factual understanding through 'who', 'what', 'where', and 'how' questions; also includes 'reference to context' questions to test in-depth understanding of the lesson

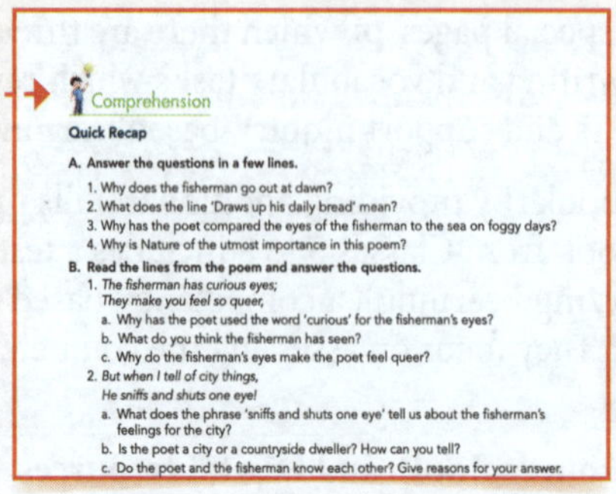

Life Skills and Values

- Inferential and extrapolative higher order thinking skills (HOTS) questions on moral values and interpersonal skills, mapped to twenty-first century skills

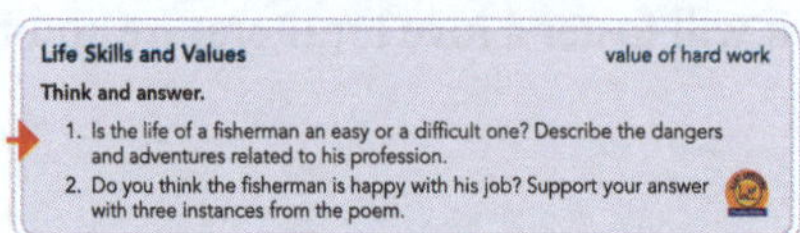

Graphic Story

- Graphic story in Classes 1-7 to aid visual learning

Glossary

- Provides contextual meanings of difficult words and phrases, given alongside the reading passage

About the author/poet

- Gives a brief biography of the writer, with names of their best known works

Literary term, Did You Know?

- Provide additional information on literary devices and figures of speech, and trivia to develop cross-curricular intelligence

Way with Words

- Includes exercises on contextual application of language encountered in the reading text
- Fosters appreciation of literary devices and figures of speech (simile, metaphor, personification, etc)

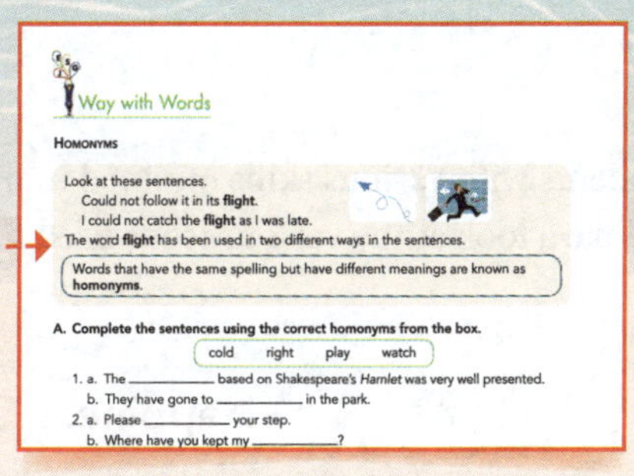

Grammar in Use

- Imparts formal understanding of language structures and syntax
- Includes easy-to-understand explanations of grammar concepts, graphic organisers and plenty of practice exercises

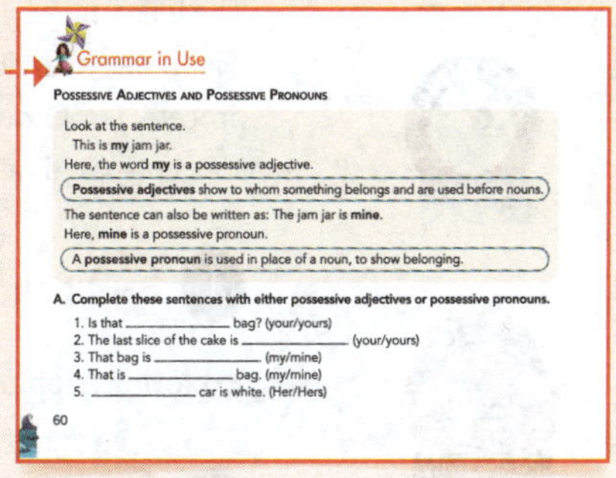

Listening and Speaking

- Facilitates fluency in oral and aural communication
- Includes conversation practice, role plays, debates and listening comprehension
- Exercises on rhyme and meter in poetry chapters

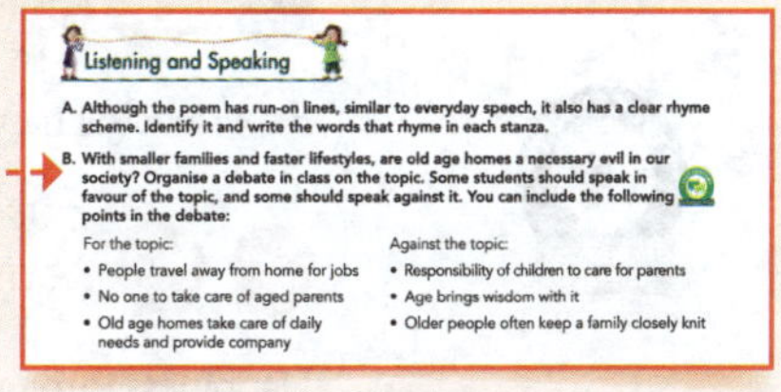

Pen it Down

- Includes guided and free writing tasks, to enable learners to express themselves creatively, logically and coherently

Now I can

- Self-assessment of learning objectives for the chapter

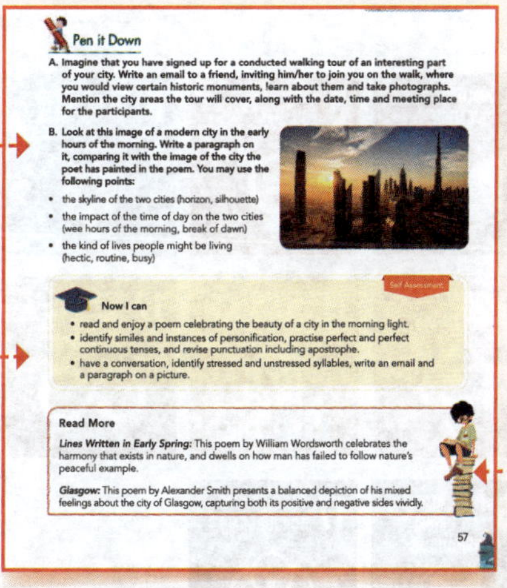

Study Skills

- Develops the sub-skills of language study
- **Spell Check** and **Pronounce Well** include phonics drills and exercises on spelling
- **Use Your Dictionary** develops dictionary referencing skills

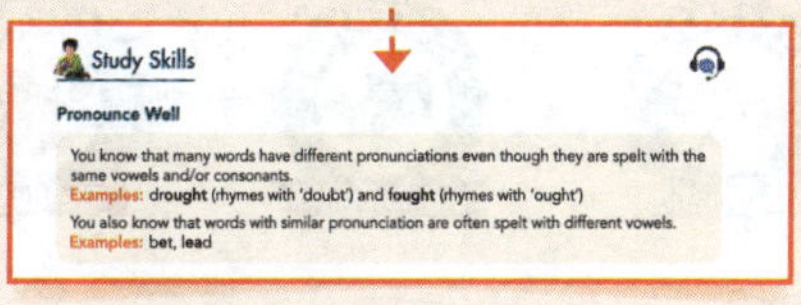

Literary Genres and Terms

- Includes a glossary to introduce literary genres and explain literary devices and narrative tools

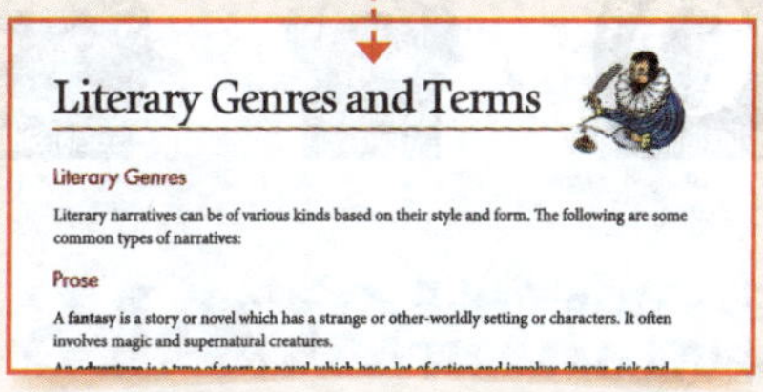

Read More

- Contains extra suggested reading for the avid learner to foster love for literature

Assessments

- Includes a Test Paper in Workbooks 3-8 based on the principle of SAFAL that encourages competency-based learning

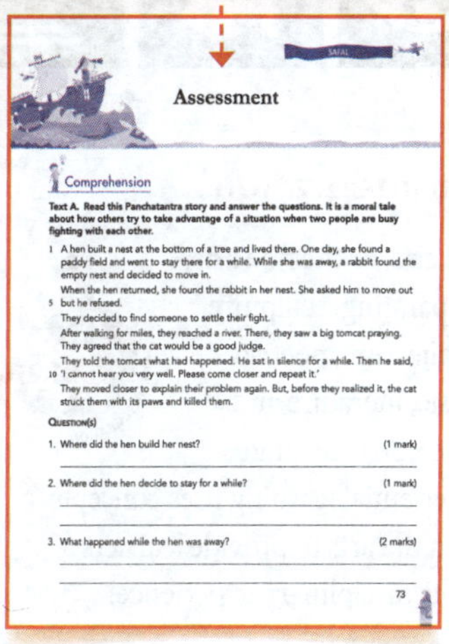

Poster

- Literature and vocabulary games, and activities based on distinct themes

Icons

Revised Engaging English aims to equip students with various skills outlined in the National Education Policy, 2020, that target the holistic education of the learner. Take a look at the various icons used to showcase these skills.

Twenty-first Century Skills

Mastering these skills will equip learners to face the challenges of a rapidly changing, digital society.

21ST CENTURY: Collaboration · Communication · Creativity · Critical Thinking · Initiative · Leadership · Media Literacy · Productivity · Flexibility · Information Literacy · Social Skills · Technology Literacy

Happiness Content

The idea underlying 'Happiness Content', a part of the 'Happiness Curriculum', is that learning should be an enjoyable process. For knowledge to bring joy, learning must focus on concept-based rather than rote learning.

1 HC **Learning and Awareness**

Exploring happiness through Learning and Awareness

2 HC **Feelings**

Experiencing happiness in relationships through Feelings

3 HC **Active Participation**

Happiness through Active Participation

SUSTAINABLE DEVELOPMENT GOALS

1 NO POVERTY · 2 ZERO HUNGER · 3 GOOD HEALTH AND WELL-BEING · 4 QUALITY EDUCATION · 5 GENDER EQUALITY · 6 CLEAN WATER AND SANITATION · 7 AFFORDABLE AND CLEAN ENERGY · 8 DECENT WORK AND ECONOMIC GROWTH · 9 INDUSTRY, INNOVATION AND INFRASTRUCTURE · 10 REDUCED INEQUALITIES · 11 SUSTAINABLE CITIES AND COMMUNITIES · 12 RESPONSIBLE CONSUMPTION AND PRODUCTION · 13 CLIMATE ACTION · 14 LIFE BELOW WATER · 15 LIFE ON LAND · 16 PEACE, JUSTICE AND STRONG INSTITUTIONS · 17 PARTNERSHIPS FOR THE GOALS

The Sustainable Development Goals (SDGs) were adopted by the United Nations in 2015 as a universal call to action to end poverty, protect the planet, and ensure that by 2030, all people enjoy peace and prosperity. The 17 SDGs recognize that development must balance social, economic and environmental sustainability.

Art Integration

The arts, or the fine arts, are painting, sculpture, architecture, poetry, music, literature and dance. Art-integrated experiential learning uses concepts from the arts to provide learners a multi-disciplinary experience.

ART INTEGRATION

Cross-curricular Content

The cross-curricular approach to teaching recognises that subjects are inter-linked, and for effective concept-acquisition, they must be taught in synergy with each other.

Did You Know? G.K.

Cows have a great sense of smell. They can smell things as far as nine kilometres away!

Math · Science · History · Geography

Acknowledgements

The publishers wish to thank and acknowledge the following for granting us permission to use copyright material:

Ruskin Bond for *A Crow in the House*. Reprinted with the permission of the author; Madhu Gurung for *The Naga Dragon's Lair* from the book, *Burmese Folktales*. Reprinted with the permission of the author; *My Elephant is Missing* copyright © 2009 Kenn Nesbitt. All Rights Reserved. Reprinted by permission of the author; *Harriet Tubman and the Underground Railroad*, written by Philip Steele and illustrated by Alexander Jansson. Reprinted by permission of HarperCollins Publishers Ltd © 2013, Philip Steele.

The publishers have applied for permission for the following:
Grandad's Gadget by Marian Swinger, *Guno and Koyo* by Kala Thairani, *Rainmaking* by Shankar, *The Recycling Rap* by John Foster, *The Sound Collector* by Roger McGough, *The Girl who Stepped on the Loaf* by Augusta Stevenson. Acknowledgements for these texts will be made in the future editions of the book.

Every effort has been made to trace copyright holders and to obtain their permission for the use of copyright material. However, in some instances, we have been unable to trace the owners of the copyright pieces published here. The authors and publishers will gladly receive any information enabling them to rectify any error or omission in subsequent editions.

Illustrations

Inside: **Page 6: SDG logo and icons:** https://www.un.org/sustainabledevelopment/
The content of this publication has not been approved by the United Nations and does not reflect the views of the United Nations or its officials or Member States. **11:** Natalie_, nicoletaionescu; **12:** johnwoodcock, tachyglossus; **15:** dedMazay; **17:** BluezAce; **19:** sabelskaya, Victor_Brave; **23:** VasjaKoman; **24:** nstanev; **26:** Macrovector, designer29, bortonia, Pavel Shubin, gmm2000, GharizaMahavira, ARTPUPPY, ET-ARTWORKS; **32:** CSA-Archive; **37:** jesadaphorn; **40:** Qvasimodo; **41:** CSA-Archive; **42:** LokFung; **46:** habun; **47:** Andrew_Howe; **48:** aqabiz; **52:** Bellott; **57:** Alina Kvaratskhelia, cgdeaw; **58:** Kharlamova; **59:** inmoon; **60:** JakeOlimb; **63:** rod2334; **67:** Aleutie; **71:** mariaflaya; **72:** nokee; **73:** zaricm; **74:** anitnov; **76:** duncan1890; **82:** dddb; **89:** sceka; **90:** VolodymyrKozin; **91:** Armation74; **96:** zak00, ChakisAtelier; **97:** artisticco; **100:** zstockll; **105:** Alefclipart; **107:** kgena1; **108:** Andesign101 ; **109:** Tigatelu; **111:** sanlas, smartboy10, bortonia, Zhe_Vasylieva; **114:** sidop, zaricm; **115:** undefined undefined; **123:** pijama61; **125:** subodhsathe, Juanmonino, arinahabich, Studio-Annika, avid_creative; **132:** colematt; **137:** kristijanh; **139:** colematt; **141:** lenm; **148:** skeeg; **150:** The Granger collection, New York; **151:** incomible.

Detailed Contents

Unit	Theme	Comprehension	Way with Words	Grammar in Use	Study Skills	Listening and Speaking	Pen it Down
1. Heidi	Home and Family	• Reference to context • Questions	• Collective nouns	• Types of sentences • Adjectives	• Spell Check: words ending with *-el* and *-al*	• Talking about one's preference	• Making a list • Letter writing
2. A Noble Dog	Physical Activities and Sports	• Questions • Reference to context	• Word meanings • Antonyms	• Simple past tense • Articles	• Spell Check: spelling similar sounding words	• Listening for sounds: stressed syllables	• Paragraph writing: narrative
3. Grandad's Gadget	Technology	• Questions • Reference to context	• Compound words • Professions	• Pronouns: personal, subject and object • Punctuation: comma, full stop, question mark, exclamation mark, capital letters	• Use Your Dictionary: contextual word meanings	• Completing a conversation	• Writing a 'Thank you' note
4. Guno and Koyo	Tales of Folly	• Questions • Reference to context	• Proverbs • Phrasal verbs	• Subject and predicate • Word forms: verbs to nouns • Punctuation: inverted comma	• Use Your Dictionary: identifying headwords	• Discussion	• Diary writing
5. Bread Making	Food and Nutrition	• Questions • Reference to context	• Prefixes	• Simple present tense • Present continuous tense	• Spell check: words ending in *-sion*, *-cian* and *-tion*	• Listening for information and answering questions	• Recipe writing
6. Rainmaking	Our Country	• Questions • Reference to context	• Contextual words • Analogies	• Adjective: degrees of comparison • Word forms: verbs and nouns	• Use Your Dictionary: finding synonyms	• Listening and discussing	• Making a list and specifying reasons • Writing an apology note
Be Creative!							
7. The Recycling Rap	Protecting the Environment	• Questions • Reference to context	• Word pairs • Making sentences	• Possessive adjectives and possessive pronouns • Main and auxiliary verbs	• Spell Check: spelling words ending with *-ar* or *-er*	• Listening and sequencing	• Notice writing
8. A Crow in the House	Neighbourhood and Community	• Questions • Reference to context	• Commonly confused words • Contextual words	• Using *which/who* to join sentences • Subject-verb agreement	• Pronounce Well: stressed letters in a word	• Listening to a passage and answering questions • Expressing one's opinion	• Paragraph writing: descriptive
9. Life Cycle of a Butterfly	Animals and Plants	• Questions • Reference to context	• Jumbled words related to butterflies • Word order in sentences	• Simple future tense	• Spell Check: spelling words ending in *-ent* and *-ant*	• Listening to the stressed and unstressed words and identifying them	• Paragraph writing: descriptive

Unit	Theme	Comprehension	Way with Words	Grammar in Use	Study Skills	Listening and Speaking	Pen it Down
10. Oliver Goes to London	The City	• Questions • Reference to context	• Synonyms • Verbs starting with the letter *r*	• Prepositions • Transitive and intransitive verbs	• Spell Check: spelling names of sports	• Listening to a discussion and expressing agreement/ disagreement	• Writing a short composition: predicting the ending of a story
11. The Naga Dragon's Lair	Southeast Asia	• Questions • Reference to context	• Similes • Objects and sounds	• Types of adjectives • Types of adverbs	• Use Your Dictionary: word meanings and sentences	• Listening and gap filling • Discussion	• Writing a short composition: personal account
12. The Sound Collector	Daily Activities	• Questions • Reference to context	• Word search: sound words • Imagery	• Past continuous tense • Mixed tenses	• Pronounce Well: words often mispronounced	• Identifying various sounds and classifying them as noise or pleasant sounds	• Writing a paragraph about feelings
Be Creative!							
13. The Wizard of Oz	Long Journeys	• Questions • Reference to context	• Word meanings • Anagrams • Binomial pairs	• Phrases • Apostrophe to show possession	• Spell Check: commonly misspelt words	• Listening to a passage and gap filling • Holding a conversation with the help of cues	• Poster making
14. The Lighthouse	By the Sea	• Questions • Reference to context	• Words related to the sea • Making new words by adding a letter	• Present and past participles	• Pronounce Well: homophones	• Listening and talking about school rules	• Making an invitation card
15. How The Leopard Got His Spots	Animal Stories	• Questions • Reference to context	• Suffixes • Adjectives: nationalitites	• Adjective phrase	• Spell Check: spelling similar sounding *oo/ue* words	• Listening to a conversation and giving advice	• Researching and writing a short paragraph
16. The Girl Who Stepped on the Loaf	Christmas Stories	• Questions • Reference to context	• Movement verbs • Crossword	• Direct and indirect speech • Error correction	• Use Your Dictionary: locating compound words	• Listening to a conversation, understanding and discussing the central theme	• Dialogue writing
17. My Elephant is Missing	Humour	• Filling the blanks • Questions	• Rhyming words • Homophones	• Apostrophe for contractions	• Pronounce Well: vowel sounds	• Listening to a poem and reciting it	• Writing a notice
18. Harriet Tubman and the Underground Railroad	Freedom and Slavery	• Questions • Reference to context	• Idioms with *catch* • Collocations: verbs and nouns	• Subject-verb agreement • Conjunctions	• Use Your Dictionary: finding meanings and answering questions	• Role play: an invitation	• Letter writing
Be Creative!							
Literary Genres and Terms							

Contents

1 Heidi

Johanna Spyri

Let's Get Started

We create special memories with people whom we grow close to. Think of three family members and two friends who are dear to you. Note down one memory you have with each of them.

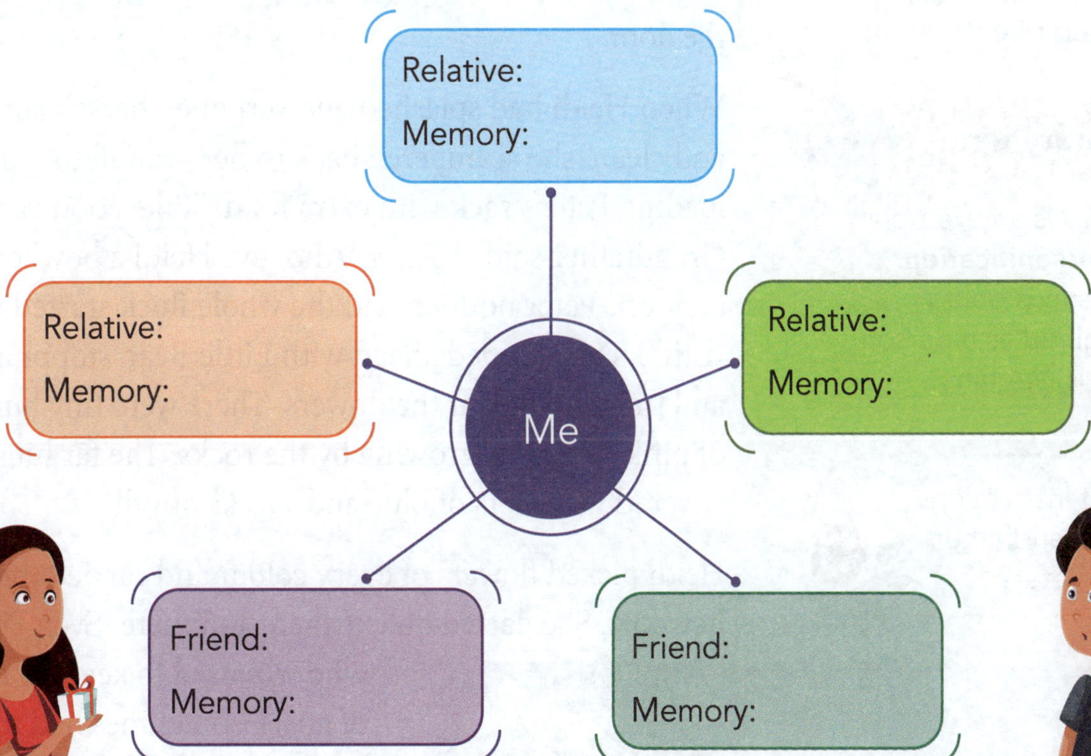

HC **Feelings:** Contributions in relationships (grandparents)

Reading

This extract is taken from* Heidi*, a novel about a young girl who comes to stay with her grandfather (nicknamed Alm-Uncle by the villagers) on a high mountain in

Switzerland. Heidi had been brought up by her aunt in the city. Do you think she will like her new life away from the city?

Heidi awoke the next morning to a **shrill** whistle. She opened her eyes and saw the sun pouring in through her window. It shone on the hay, making it look like a pile of gold. For a moment, Heidi was not sure where she was. Then she heard her grandfather's voice outside and it all came back to her. She jumped out of bed quickly, dressed and **scrambled** down the ladder.

shrill: sharp
scrambled: moved quickly, using one's hands
scampered: ran with light steps
trail: path or route
specks: tiny spots
darted: moved suddenly and quickly
nibbled: took small, repeated bites

Peter and his flock were already outside. Little Swan and Little Bear were just coming out of their goat hut with Grandfather. Heidi ran over to wish them all good morning. 'Would you like to go climbing with Peter and the goats?' Grandfather asked. Heidi jumped with joy. 'Go and wash first, or else the sun will laugh at you.'[1] Grandfather pointed to a bucket of fresh water waiting by the door.

Literary term

1. This is an example of **personification**. The sun is being imagined as a person who is laughing.

When Heidi had splashed and scrubbed herself shiny and clean, she **scampered** back to her grandfather. He was loading Peter's sack with extra food. 'Take good care,' Grandfather said to Peter. 'And give Heidi a bowl of milk at noon.' Peter nodded and the whole flock started up the **trail**. Heidi skipped ahead with Little Bear, stopping here and there to look at the flowers. There were tiny bunches of pink blossoms growing by the rocks. The far hills were covered with dots of blue and **specks** of yellow.

What instructions did Grandfather give Peter?

Heidi picked flowers of every colour and carried them in her skirt. She **darted** quickly here and there. Even Peter, who was used to keeping track of goats, sometimes had trouble finding her. 'If you pick them all, there won't be any left for tomorrow,' Peter laughed. The flock climbed up until they came to a meadow at the base of a high cliff. Here the goats **nibbled** on herbs and grasses as Peter

stretched out to rest under the sun. Heidi put her flowers in the lunch bag and took a good look around.

The wide valley **yawned** below. Above, the **jagged** mountaintops stretched into the blue sky. Heidi sat very still, watching the wind play with the grasses and flower stems. She drank in the sunshine and felt wonderfully happy. Sometime later, a large blackbird circled high overhead. His **piercing** cry woke Peter and he began to unpack their lunch.

While Peter milked Little Swan, Heidi jumped about with the goats. 'Stop your jumping, and come and eat,' Peter called when Heidi's bowl was full of milk. Heidi was so excited that she could not eat all of the bread and cheese her grandfather had packed for her. When she had eaten her fill, she pushed the rest over to Peter. 'You may have the rest. I am full.' Peter's eyes grew wide. He was not sure what to say. Never in his life had he been full enough to give food away. He was not sure he should take it. 'Please,' Heidi said, 'it's for you.' Peter smiled and took a bite. It was delicious. Soon his belly was as full as Heidi's.

He settled back to watch Heidi play with the goats. 'What are the goats' names?' Heidi asked him. Peter knew them all. Though he was only eleven, he had been **herding** the goats for several years. He collected them each morning in Little Village and took them home again each night. While Heidi darted back and forth among them, he called out the name of each goat.

There was Turk with huge horns, who was always **butting** the smaller goats. There was Fink, who was brave. He ran at Turk again and again, even though he was only half of Turk's size. And there was also a little goat that would bleat and bleat so much that Heidi put her arms around her. That was Hopli. 'Why does she cry?' Heidi asked Peter. 'Because her mother was sold and doesn't come up the mountain anymore,' Peter explained. 'Don't cry,' Heidi told Hopli. 'I will come up with you every day. Then you won't

Where did Heidi keep the flowers?

yawned: (here) opened wide

jagged: rough and uneven

piercing: loud and shrill

herding: making animals move together in a group

butting: hitting with horns

Did You Know? Geography

Switzerland is a country in Europe. It is famous for chocolates, cheese and watchmaking. The Alps cover a large part of the country.

How old was Peter?

heart leaped: had a sudden feeling of excitement or happiness

rapidly: quickly

Did You Know? Geography

The Alm is the seasonal pastureland for grazing in the Alps mountains in Switzerland. In summer, animals are herded to the valleys, while in winter, they are taken to the plains.

Why was Grandfather sitting outside the hut?

be lonely.' The little goat quietened down and rubbed her head on Heidi's shoulder.

Of all the goats, Little Swan and Little Bear were the finest. Even Peter thought so. 'They are the finest because Alm-Uncle brushes them and washes them and gives them the best shed,' he said with a nod. All too soon, the light began to change. The snow, high on the hills, turned rosy red, and the blackbird returned to circle and cry. Peter started down the mountain but Heidi did not want to. It had been a perfect and beautiful day, and she was sad to see it go. But she followed Peter and the goats down the mountain to her grandfather's house.

Grandfather was sitting outside his hut, waiting for the flock to return. Little Swan and Little Bear ran to see their master and licked the salt he held for them in his hand. 'Did you have fun, Heidi?' Grandfather asked.

'Oh, yes,' Heidi told him. 'I will forever remember what I saw today.'

'But you can see it all again tomorrow, Heidi,' Peter said.

Heidi's **heart leaped**. She looked at her grandfather hopefully. 'May I? May I really, Grandfather?'

'Of course,' her grandfather laughed. 'You may go up the mountain every day until winter.'

Heidi jumped up and down. She hugged Little Swan and Peter and talked **rapidly** to her grandfather.

'Oh, it is so wonderful up there!' she cried. 'There are so many flowers and a blackbird and snow on the mountaintops that turns red in the sunlight.'

Then Grandfather smiled and pointed Heidi toward the washtub. 'Yes, yes,' he said. 'Now, why don't you go and bathe? I'll fetch the milk and you can tell me all about it over supper.'

About the author

Johanna Spyri (1827–1901) was a children's author born in Switzerland. She is best known for her novel, *Heidi*, one of the most popular books of Swiss literature. It has been translated from German into 50 languages and filmed multiple times.

Comprehension

Quick Recap

A. Read the lines from the extract and answer the questions.

1. *'Go and wash first, or else the sun will laugh at you.'*
   a. Who said these words and to whom?
   b. Why did the speaker want her to wash first?
   c. Where was she going?
2. *'I will come up with you every day.'*
   a. Who said these words and to whom?
   b. Why did the speaker say these words?
   c. What was the creature's response?

B. Answer the questions.

1. What awoke Heidi in the morning?
2. Who was waiting outside the hut?
3. What did Heidi do while climbing up the mountain?
4. What did Heidi, Peter and the goats do when they came to a meadow at the base of a high cliff?
5. What were the names of the goats that Peter herded? Describe them.
6. Why were Little Swan and Little Bear the finest among all the goats?
7. Which lines in the extract suggest that the day was coming to an end?
8. What did Little Swan and Little Bear do when they reached Grandfather's hut?

Life Skills and Values — learning to share

Think and answer.

1. How do we know that Heidi enjoyed her day out with Peter and the goats?
2. Do you think Heidi was a generous girl? Give reasons for your answer.
3. What kind of a boy was Peter? Write a few lines about him.

21st Century Critical Thinking

Way with Words

Collective Nouns

In the extract, Peter takes a herd of goats to the mountains to graze. The word **herd** is a collective noun used to refer to goats.

A. Complete the phrases using suitable collective nouns from the box.

herd	pride	bunch	troupe	band	pack	crowd	choir

1. a ________________ of keys
2. a ________________ of elephants
3. a ________________ of cards
4. a ________________ of singers
5. a ________________ of people
6. a ________________ of dancers
7. a ________________ of lions
8. a ________________ of musicians

B. Complete the phrases with collective nouns for words used in the passage.

1. a ______________________ of sheep
2. a ______________________ of birds
3. a ______________________ of flowers
4. a ______________________ of grass
5. a ______________________ of trees
6. a ______________________ of mountains

Grammar in Use

Types of Sentences

A **sentence** is a group of words that makes sense and expresses a complete thought.

There are four types of sentences. Look at these examples.

1. Peter and his flock were already outside.
   This is an **assertive sentence**, which says or states something.
2. Did you have fun, Heidi?
   This is an **interrogative sentence**, which asks a question.
3. Take good care and give Heidi a bowl of milk at noon.
   This is an **imperative sentence**, which gives an order or makes a request.
4. Watch out!
   This is an **exclamatory sentence**, which is used to express surprise, anger and other strong emotions.

A. **State whether these sentences are assertive, interrogative, imperative or exclamatory.**

1. Raman is a mischievous boy. ________________
2. Oh, what a beautiful painting! ________________
3. Do you like to watch cricket? ________________
4. New Delhi is the capital of India. ________________
5. Hurrah, we won the match! ________________
6. Where are you going? ________________
7. Please pass me the salt. ________________
8. Have you done your homework? ________________

B. **Arrange the words to make meaningful sentences. Remember to include the correct punctuation marks. Then, circle the interrogative sentences.**

1. like/playing/I/my/with/sister/baby
2. is/colour/what/favourite/your
3. a/lovely/what/day
4. know/my/do/pencil/you/is/where
5. a/request/strange/what
6. lend/book/please/me/today/your

ADJECTIVES

You know that adjectives are describing words. They are used to describe nouns.

Examples: Grandfather pointed to a bucket of **fresh** water waiting by the door.
A **large** <u>blackbird</u> circled overhead.

C. **Read this paragraph about a puppy. Underline the adjectives and circle the nouns they describe.**

Caesar is a playful puppy. It has white fur and a fluffy, curly tail. The red leash around its neck makes it look cute. Caesar comes to the park every evening and plays with the small children. It barks at the naughty kids who try to frighten it.

Study Skills

Spell Check

Look at these words.

towel **usual**

Although 'towel' ends with **-el** and 'usual' ends with **-al**, the two words are pronounced in the same way. Spellings of words ending with **-al** and **-el** are, hence, often confused.

Add the letters -el or -al to complete these words. You can use your dictionary to check the spelling.

1. carniv ________ 3. coast ________ 5. norm ________
2. chann ________ 4. tunn ________ 6. glob ________

Listening and Speaking

Listen to Rohit talk about what he wants to do. Imagine that your parents have given you a choice – to either go for a swim with your friends or go shopping with them. Speak about what you would like to do. Give reasons for your choice.

You can use phrases like:

- I would like to...
- I want/don't want to...
- This is because...

Pen it Down

A. You are going on a trip with your friends to the mountains. You have to carry only the essential things. Work in pairs and make a list of ten things that you would need for the trip. Give reasons for each item that you will carry with you.

B. Imagine that you are Heidi. Write a letter to your aunt in the city describing your life in the mountains with Grandfather, using these points:

- Grandfather's behaviour
- the mountains
- experience of going to the pasture with Peter to graze the goats

Self Assessment

Now I can

- understand a story about a little girl who learns to appreciate nature.
- recognize collective nouns, different types of sentences, and adjectives.
- speak about my choices, make a detailed list, and write a letter to a relative.

Read More

The Faraway Tree: This book by Enid Blyton is about the adventures of Joe, Bessie and Fanny, three children who come to live near an enchanted forest with a magical tree.

The Railway Children: This book by Edith Nesbit is about three children, who go to live in a village in England after their father is wrongly arrested. The children play along the railway lines, have many adventures and stop a train accident.

short story

2
A Noble Dog

Edith Nesbit

Let's Get Started

Do you know how to swim? Read these safety rules for swimming. Tick [✓] the ones which you think are correct. Put a cross [×] for the ones which you think are incorrect.

☐ Be careful while entering or leaving the pool.

☐ You can swim alone without a grown-up present.

☐ Wear a life vest if you are a beginner.

☐ Follow the instructions of the coach or lifeguard.

☐ You can play games in which you have to hold your breath.

Match the signs with the rules that we should follow at the beach.

Signs	Rules
 •	• no pets allowed at the beach
 •	• first-aid available
 •	• use an umbrella
 •	• no littering on the beach
 •	• use changing rooms

HC **Learning and Awareness:** Clarity of purpose

Reading

Why do you think people keep pets like dogs and cats at home? Read a story about two

Why would Rover go into the water?

bound: run
vain: proud
superior: better
prize: highly valued
humble: (here) not of a high rank or status
nettled: made angry
meekness: (here) unwillingness to join others in an activity

Did You Know? G.K.

The Newfoundland breed of dog comes from the Newfoundland island, in Canada. The large, intelligent and obedient dog is used to rescue people who are drowning.

Why did the dogs spend time by the river?

pet dogs of different breeds and their special relationship with their human family.

Rover would go into the water fast enough for a bath or a swim, but he would not bring anything out. The children used to throw in sticks, and Rover and I used to **bound** in together. But I would bring the sticks back, while he swam round and round, enjoying himself.

I am not **vain**, but I could not help feeling how much **superior** I was to such a dog as Rover. He is a **prize** Newfoundland, and I am only a **humble** retriever of unknown family.

So one day I said to him, 'Why don't you fetch the sticks out when the children throw them in?'

'I don't care about sticks,' he said.

'But it's so grand and clever to be able to fetch them out.'

'Is it?' he answered.

'I know it is, for the children tell me so.'

'Do they?' he said.

'I wonder you are not ashamed,' I went on, a little **nettled** by his **meekness**, 'never to do anything useful. I should be, if I were you.'

'Ah,' he said, 'but you see, you are not. Good night.'

We used to spend a great deal of time by the river. The children loved to play there and we dogs were always expected to go with them.

One day, as I was lying asleep on the warm grass by the river bank, I heard a splash. I jumped in, but there was no stick, only one of the children floating down on the stream and screaming whenever her head came up from under the water.

I thought it was a new kind of game, which was not very interesting. So I swam out again. Just as I was shaking the water out of my ears, I heard another great flop and there was Rover in the water, holding on to the child's dress. He pulled her out some ten yards down the stream. And oh! If you could have seen the fuss that the master and mistress, and the rest of the children made of that black and white spotted person!

mild: gentle

'Why, Rover,' I said afterwards, when we had got home and were talking it over, 'Whatever made you think that the child wanted to be pulled out of the water?'

Why did Rover jump into the water?

'It's my business to pull people out of the water,' he said.

'But,' I said 'I always thought you were too foolish to understand things.'

'Did you?' he said, turning his **mild** eyes on me.

'Why didn't you explain to me that you—'

'My dear dog,' he said, 'I never think it worthwhile to fetch sticks out of the water and I never think it worthwhile to explain things to foolish people.'

About the author

Edith Nesbit (1858–1924) was an English writer and poet who wrote poems, short stories and novels. Among her best-known books are *The Story of the Treasure Seekers* and *The Wouldbegoods*, a tale about a family facing hard times.

Comprehension

Quick Recap

A. Answer the questions in a few lines.

1. Who is the narrator of this story?
2. Who is Rover? How did the narrator know him?
3. When the children threw sticks in the water, how did the two animals react?

4. Why did the narrator fetch the sticks thrown by the children?
5. Why did the narrator feel that Rover should be ashamed of himself?
6. Why did the narrator swim out of the river soon after jumping in?
7. How did Rover behave in the same situation?

B. Read the lines from the story and answer the questions.

1. *I am not vain, but I could not help feeling how much superior I was to such a dog as Rover.*
   a. Who said that he was not vain?
   b. Why did he feel superior to Rover?
   c. Was the speaker really superior to Rover? Give a reason for your answer.
2. *... I went on, a little nettled by his meekness ...*
   a. Who was nettled by whose meekness? Why?
   b. What does the word 'meekness' mean here?
   c. What did the speaker say to the other dog?
3. *'I never think it worthwhile to fetch sticks out of the water and I never think it worthwhile to explain things to foolish people.'*
   a. Who said these words?
   b. Who was the speaker referring to as 'foolish people'?
   c. Why did the speaker say these words?

Life Skills and Values selflessness, alertness

Think and answer.

1. What kind of dog is Rover shown to be?
2. The word 'noble' refers to certain qualities. Who do you think is the noble dog of the story?

21st Century Leadership

Way with Words

A. Write the meanings of the following words from the story. Take the help of a dictionary, if needed.

1. flop	2. worthwhile	3. grand
4. expected	5. fuss	6. stream

Antonyms

B. Find the antonyms of the following words from the story.

1. slow ____________________
2. inferior ____________________
3. proud ____________________
4. known ____________________
5. foolish ____________________
6. willingness ____________________
7. push ____________________
8. useless ____________________

Grammar in Use

Simple Past Tense

Read the sentences.

The children **loved** to play there.

The dogs **followed** the children.

The words **loved** and **followed** are in the simple past tense.

The **simple past tense** describes an action that has been completed in the past.

A. Underline the words in the simple past tense in the passage.

The children watched the magic show quietly. The magician brought a big box on the stage. He walked into it and closed the lid. Nothing happened for five minutes. A girl went up and opened the box but found it empty. The magician had disappeared. The children were very surprised.

B. Fill in the blanks with the simple past tense of the following words.

1. My mother ________________ my dinner to the bedroom. (bring)
2. The school bell ________________ at the end of the last period. (ring)
3. Last week, my friend and I ________________ to school every day. (walk)
4. Grandfather ________________ me a new pair of socks. (give)
5. My sister ________________ a chocolate cake for my birthday. (bake)
6. The prince ________________ Cinderella's missing slipper. (find)

Articles are used to define a noun. **A, an** and **the** are articles.

A and **an** are called **indefinite articles** and are used while talking about a singular countable noun or when a noun is being referred to for the first time. **A** is used before nouns that begin with a consonant sound and **an** is used before nouns that begin with a vowel sound.

The is called the **definite article** and is used to talk about a specific noun.

Examples:

I thought it was **a** new kind of game.
Here **a** refers to 'game'.
The children would throw the stick for them.
Here **the** refers to a definite noun which is 'children'.

C. Complete the sentences using articles.

1. ______________ apple a day keeps the doctor away.
2. She is ______________ teacher in a school.
3. We saw ______________ Gateway of India in Mumbai.
4. I trust him because he is ______________ honest man.
5. ______________ peacock is ______________ national bird of India.
6. I have bought ______________ new game. Do you want to play it with me?

Study Skills

Spell Check

We often misspell words when we miss a letter while writing in a hurry.
We also make mistakes when we confuse the spelling of words with the same sound.
Example: night, knight

Underline the words in the passage that are not spelled correctly. Write their correct spelling.

One day Rohan decided to make a flute out of a peice of bamboo. He wondred if he could make some holes in it. First he thought that he wood play some tunes on it. Then he relized that it would make an intersting telescope. He raized it to one eye and saw an eagle flying towads him.

Listening and Speaking

A **syllable** is a word, or a part of a word, that contains a single vowel sound (*a*, *e*, *i*, *o*, *u*).

A word can contain one or more syllables. When we have two-syllable words, only one syllable is spoken with more force – either the first syllable or the second one.

Examples: **cof**fee, **ex**it (stress on the first syllable)
a**bout**, be**cause** (stress on the second syllable)

Listen to these words that stress on the first syllable and say them aloud.

PRESent, EXport, CHIna, TAble, SLENder, CLEVer, HAPpy

Now, think of five more words that stress on the first syllable. Write them and practise saying them aloud in class.

Pen it Down

Imagine that you have a pet of your own. Write a paragraph about an unusual experience with your pet.

You can use these points in your paragraph:

- how you got your pet
- what your pet looks like, its behaviour and habits
- whether the unusual incident changed your views about your pet

Self Assessment

Now I can

- read a story about two dogs and understand the meaning of the word 'noble'.
- use the simple past tense and revise antonyms and articles.
- practise saying words with stress on the first syllable and write a paragraph.

Read More

The Loyal Mongoose: This story, taken from *The Tales of Panchatantra*, brings out the extraordinary loyalty of a pet mongoose.

Hachiko — The True Story of a Loyal Dog: This famous story from Japan by Pamela S. Turner is about the feelings of devotion, love and trust that Hachiko, the dog, shows for his master.

3

Grandad's Gadget

light verse

Technology

Marian Swinger

Let's Get Started

SUSTAINABLE DEVELOPMENT GOALS

The United Nations Sustainable Development Goal 9 aims to come up with technologies that do not harm the environment and help us coexist with Nature.

A technology is any method or machine where we use science for day-to-day activities. Write the names of the modern items in the right column that were inspired by the old technologies in the left column.

Old technology	New technology
fire-making 	
sundial 	
typewriter 	
telephone 	

HC **Feelings:** Contributions in relationships (siblings and grandparents)

Reading

Read about a little boy and his talented grandfather. The grandfather builds a strange

gadget: machine

tweezers: a small tool with two long thin parts joined at one end and used to pick up small objects

mend: repair

queue: line

battered: damaged

twinkling: shining

machine that can repair old and broken toys.

Grandad built a **gadget** made of
tweezers, hooks and springs.

'My little gadget,' Grandad said,
'can **mend** just anything.

So bring your broken toys along,
broken china too.

Then press this button. My machine
will make them good as new!'

We brought a pile of toys along.
My best friend brought a bike.[1]

'That's right,' said Grandad, 'form a **queue**.
Bring anything you like.'

But the gadget built more gadgets from
the broken, **battered** toys
which ran about on little legs
around the girls and boys.

Then they rushed at Grandad
on their tiny, **twinkling** feet
and Grandad hopped and shouted as
they chased him down the street.

Literary term

1. This is an example of **alliteration**. The 'b' sound is repeated at the beginning of these words: 'My best friend brought a bike.'

With what did the new gadgets chase Grandad?

Did You Know? G.K.

China is a type of white clay used for making beautiful cups and plates. This technique, called ceramics, was invented in China.

Comprehension

Quick Recap

A. Answer the questions in a few lines.

1. What did Grandad build?
2. What did he use to build it?
3. What did the speaker and his friends bring?
4. What was Grandad's gadget supposed to do?
5. What did the gadget actually do?
6. What did the new gadgets do?
7. Make a list of the rhyming words in the poem.

B. Read the lines from the poem and answer the questions.

1. *'My machine will make them good as new!'*
   a. Who said these words?
   b. What would become 'good as new'?
   c. What had to be done to 'make them good as new'?
2. *'Then they rushed at Grandad...'*
   a. Who does 'they' refer to?
   b. What was Grandad's reaction?
   c. Where did 'they' chase him to?

Life Skills and Values — humour, innovation

Think and answer.

1. Why do you think the tiny new gadgets ran around the girls and boys, and chased Grandad?
2. Do you think the poem is funny? If you do, make a list of the things that you find funny in the poem.

21ST CENTURY Technology Literacy

Way with Words

Compound Words

You have learned that compound words are formed by combining two words.
Example: any + thing = anything

A. Write a word in the middle column that can be an ending for the first word and the beginning for the second word. One has been done for you.

	centre word	
under	*ground*	*work*
fire		power
sign		room
back		knob
arm		man
ever		house

Professions

In the poem, Grandad was a scientist. A scientist is someone who studies the various natural sciences.

B. Complete these sentences describing various professions.

1. A person who designs and builds engines, machines and roads is an e ________.
2. A person who takes care of patients in a hospital is a n ________.
3. A person who is in charge of a library is a l ________.
4. A person who looks after people's teeth is a d ________.
5. A person who works on a ship is a s ________.
6. A person who repairs cars and motorcycles is a m ________.

Grammar in Use

PRONOUNS

You know that pronouns are words which are used in place of nouns to avoid repetition.

Personal pronouns are used to refer to people or things.

Subject pronouns are used as the subject of the verb and **object pronouns** are used as the object of the verb.

Type	Pronouns
Subject Pronouns	I, you, he, she, it, they, we, you
Object Pronouns	me, you, him, her, it, them, us

A. Complete the sentences with the correct pronouns.

1. After ________ (I/me) ate my dinner, I washed my hands properly.
2. My naughty brother tried to pour water on ________ (I/me).
3. Our teacher said that ________ (us/we) should not talk loudly in class.
4. They wanted ________ (us/we) to join the football match.
5. Putul went to see the doctor because ________ (she/it) was sick.
6. The boy was crying as ________ (he/his) was hungry.

PUNCTUATION

Punctuation marks are very important as they help us read a sentence correctly and make its meaning clear to us. Some important punctuation marks are the comma, full stop, question mark, exclamation mark and capital letters.

The **comma** is used to separate ideas, words or the parts of a sentence.

Examples:

After this class, we will go out to play in the park.

I had an egg, toast, butter and coffee for breakfast.

The **full stop** is used at the end of the sentence to show that the sentence is complete.

Examples:

I gave money to the shopkeeper**.**

My teacher praised me for my interesting project**.**

A **question mark** is used at the end of a sentence to show a direct question.

Examples:

When will you return my book**?**

How far is the station from your house**?**

An **exclamation mark** is used at the end of a sentence to show a strong emotion or feeling.

Examples:

What a beautiful painting**!**

What a terrible tragedy it is**!**

Capital Letters are used at the beginning of a sentence, for a proper noun and when the word 'I' is used in the middle of a sentence.

Examples:

There are eight apples in the basket.

My best friend's name is **R**oma.

My mother and **I** went to the market.

B. Rewrite the sentences using correct punctuation. You may have to add capital letters, inverted commas, question marks, exclamation marks and full stops.

1. I am going to new zealand on a holiday
2. Were you speaking to me sorry i didnt hear you
3. You naughty boy why have you broken your new toy
4. Happy new year
5. Every year I buy two dresses five pairs of shoes a new board game and a book
6. Hurry up We will be late

Study Skills

Use Your Dictionary

Look up a dictionary to find the meaning of the words in bold and answer the questions.

1. If you are asked to hold a **palette**, what would you be holding?
2. If your socks **reek**, what should you do?

3. If you feel **weary** after a long journey, what should you do?
4. If the doctor used a **rhinoscope** to examine a patient, which part of the body would he look at?
5. If you are **marooned** on an island, what should you do?

Listening and Speaking

Listen to a conversation between two people who are watching Grandad being chased by the gadgets. Complete the conversation. Then, along with a partner, enact it in front of the class, using appropriate expressions.

David: Do you know who that gentleman on the street is?
Doris: I think he is our neighbour, Mr Wilson.
David: What are those little things running on the ground?
Doris: I don't know. I am also trying to see what they are.
David: He looks a bit worried.
Doris: Mr Wilson is always trying to make new things. I wonder if it is one of his experiments gone wrong.

Pen it Down

21ST CENTURY Communication

Imagine that you are one of the children in the poem and that Grandad built a gadget for you out of your broken toys. Write a 'thank you' note to him for the gadget.

You can include the following points:

- which toy of yours it is made of
- what the gadget does
- why it makes you happy

Self Assessment

Now I can

- read a poem about recycling old objects to make new gadgets.
- recognize different professions, practise compound words and pronouns, and use punctuation marks.
- complete a conversation and write a 'thank you' note.

Read More

The Marvellous Homework and Housework Machine: This poem by Kenn Nesbitt is about a machine that can do homework and household tasks for children so that they don't get into trouble with their parents and teachers.

Time Machine: This poem by Steve Hanson is about a time machine that takes people back in time, but always makes them do a chore.

4

Guno and Koyo

Let's Get Started

Read the sentences. Tick [✓] the ones which you think are wise actions. Cross out [✗] the ones which you think are foolish.

1. Zainab wants to play with her friends in the evening. She completes her homework in the afternoon so that she is free later. [ ]
2. Joe is late for school, but he stops to talk with a friend on the way. [ ]
3. Radha receives a gift of a box of chocolates for her birthday. She knows that she should not be eating them all at the same time, but they are so delicious that she eats them all. [ ]
4. Amanpreet receives ₹ 100 as pocket money every week. Of this, she saves ₹ 20. [ ]

HC **Learning and Awareness:** Recognizing what we like versus what is good for us

Reading

Have you ever done something foolish but didn't realise it at the time? Guno and Koyo are two friends who act foolishly and get into trouble. Read this story to find out if they find a way out of the situation.

Guno and Koyo are two names known to everyone in Indonesia. Whenever their names are mentioned, people cannot hide their smiles, for Guno means 'helpful', but he is really very unhelpful. Koyo means 'wealth' but he **rarely** has any money. What is more, if Koyo ever finds any riches, his friend, Guno the helpful helps him lose it.

It happened once that Guno and Koyo decided to rob an old Hadji. In the darkness of the night, they entered noiselessly into the Hadji's **compound** and began to dig a hole in the wall.

When the hole was big enough for one man to crawl through, Guno went inside, lit a candle and by its dim light, collected the Hadji's valuables and passed them through the opening to Koyo who piled them neatly on the ground. As Guno was about to leave, his eye fell on the Hadji's colourful robe hanging on a **peg**. He removed it and tried it on himself.

'Oh, it is grand. I must not spoil it,' he told himself, feeling the rich material with his hands. Seeing the Hadji sound asleep, he decided to leave by the front door. He **tiptoed** to the door, unlocked it and went out.

Meanwhile Koyo was waiting **anxiously** for Guno's return. He sat guarding the opening they had dug and wondered why his friend was taking so long inside. Just then, he saw a **robed figure** step out from the front door. He thought it was the Hadji.

'Oh, the Hadji!' he screamed in fright and fled, leaving behind their pile of **loot**.

The robed figure was none other than Guno. When he heard Koyo's frightened **exclamation**, he thought that the Hadji had awakened and was right behind him. So, he

Wordwise

A Hadji is a Muslim man who has completed his Hajj. The Hajj is an annual pilgrimage to the holy city of Mecca in Saudi Arabia that Muslims must go for, at least once in their lifetime. A Muslim woman who has done the Hajj is called a Hajjah.

Who tried on the Hadji's robe?

rarely: not very often

compound: an area surrounded by a fence or a wall in which a group of buildings stand

peg: a nail or pin used for hanging things

tiptoed: walked quietly on one's toes

anxiously: worriedly

robed figure: a person wearing a robe

loot: stolen goods

exclamation: cry of surprise

fleeing: running away
culprits: someone who has broken a law
wailed: cried loudly from sadness or pain
in flood: close to overflowing its banks

Why did the Hadji's neighbours rush out with sticks?

threw down the robe and ran after Koyo as fast as his legs could carry him.

The two men made so much noise **fleeing** through the village that the neighbours woke up and rushed out with sticks to beat the **culprits**.

Guno and Koyo ran, too afraid to stop and look back. They ran through the village and across the open rice fields until they came to the edge of the river.

'Quick! Jump in,' said Guno.

'We are finished,' **wailed** Koyo. 'If we jump in, we shall be drowned. If we don't, the villagers will catch us and kill us.'

'Don't be a coward,' Guno said. 'The river is not **in flood**. We won't be drowned.'

'If it were in flood,' he said, 'the water would be muddy. But it is so clear, you can see the bottom of the river.'

Koyo leaned forward to take a proper look. In the faint starlight he could see the rocky surface of the riverbed.

'You may be right,' he agreed. 'But you go in first and tell me how it is.'

So Guno pulled himself up, breathed deeply, closed his eyes and leaped from the edge.

He landed on an absolutely dry bed. The stones hurt his feet, but he did not cry. Instead, he lay down and made swimming movements to make his friend believe that there was nothing to fear.

Koyo shouted, 'Why don't you say something? Is it all right?'

'Can't you see me swimming?' Guno said. 'The water is very cool.'

The villagers were close to the river now and Koyo could hear the **clanging** of their weapons. He took a deep breath, closed his eyes and jumped.

Like Guno, he landed on the dry riverbed and the stones hurt his feet and knees.

'Oo-ho! Where is the water?' he said.

'Shut up, you fool. Try and swim like me. Otherwise they will follow us here,' Guno replied.

So Koyo also stretched himself on the ground and moved his legs and arms as though he was swimming.

The villagers had now reached the riverbed. Looking down, they gazed in wonder at the two frightened men trying to swim in the river that had been dry for months.

'Look, look,' they said to each other, amazed beyond belief. Then they laughed and put down their weapons. They decided not to punish such silly **fugitives**.

Guno and Koyo had stopped 'swimming' and were now looking up fearfully at their would-be **captors**.

'Come out of the riverbed, you fools,' one of the villagers cried, giving Guno a helping hand.

After learning about Guno and Koyo's attempt to rob the Hadji, they laughed some more and sent them on their way.

'Why couldn't you have found a real river?' Koyo **grumbled**, after the villagers had left.

'Why couldn't you swim in a more believable way?' Guno replied, as he examined his **bruises**.

Did You Know? Science

In Indonesia, men wear *batik* shirts and women wear *kebaya*, an embroidered upper garment.

Batik is a cloth made using a tie-dyeing technique from India.

Which parts of his body did Koyo hurt on the dry riverbed?

clanging: loud metallic sound

fugitives: people in hiding

captors: (here) people who catch others, such as thieves

grumbled: complained in an angry but low voice

bruises: cuts

bicker: argue about silly matters

The friends continued to **bicker** as they walked back home through the moonlit fields.

Since then, whenever someone in the village tried to get out of a difficult situation by a foolish act, people would tell him, 'Don't go swimming in a dry riverbed.'

Comprehension

Quick Recap

A. Answer these questions.

1. Whom did Guno and Koyo decide to rob?
2. What did they do after reaching the Hadji's compound?
3. What problem did they face while standing on the edge of the river?
4. What did Guno do after he leaped from the edge and why?
5. Why did the villagers put away their weapons?
6. What did Guno and Koyo fight about on their walk back home?

B. Read the lines from the story and answer the questions.

1. *'Oh, it is grand. I must not spoil it,'*
   a. Who said these words?
   b. What does 'it' refer to?
   c. Who did 'it' belong to and what did the speaker do with it?
2. *'Shut up, you fool. Try and swim like me. Otherwise they will follow us here,'*
   a. Who said these words and to whom?
   b. What were the speaker and the one being spoken to doing?
   c. Who were following them and why?

Life Skills and Values

common sense, humour

Think and answer.

1. What kind of people were Guno and Koyo? Write three sentences about each of them.
2. What do you think the proverb 'Don't go swimming in a dry riverbed' means?
3. Did you think the story was funny? Mention two things in the story that made you laugh.

Way with Words

Proverbs

A **proverb** is a short, popular statement that tell us a universal truth or gives a piece of advice.

Example: Don't go swimming in a dry riverbed.

A. Match the proverbs with their meanings.

Proverbs	Meanings
1. All's well that ends well. •	• a. Foolish people speak the most.
2. A stitch in time saves nine. •	• b. Eating an apple as well as healthy foods every day will keep us healthy.
3. Honesty is the best policy. •	• c. A happy result makes us forget the problems we faced along the way.
4. An apple a day keeps the doctor away. •	• d. It is better to deal with a problem when it begins so that it doesn't get worse.
5. Empty vessels make the most noise. •	• e. Being too interested about others will land you in trouble.
6. Curiosity killed the cat. •	• f. It is always better to speak the truth than to lie.

Phrasal Verbs

A **phrasal verb** is a group of words that has a meaning which is totally different from the meaning of the individual words in it. It is usually made up of a verb and a preposition or an adverb.

Examples: **try on** (something): wear a piece of clothing to see if it fits you
get out of: escape from or avoid

B. Fill in the blanks with suitable phrasal verbs given in the box.

run out	give up	take off	switch off
look forward to	do without	turn down	catch up

1. I ______________ going back to school after a vacation.

2. The teacher realised that she had ______________ of chalk.
3. The music is very loud. Please ______________ the volume.
4. In today's world, people cannot ______________ their mobile phones.
5. He failed many times, but he did not ______________.
6. When you enter the house, please ______________ your shoes at the door.
7. You need to run faster if you want to ______________ with Sam.
8. Oliver forgot to ______________ the lights again tonight.

Grammar in Use

Subject and Predicate

You know that a sentence is made up of a subject and a predicate.

The **subject** in a sentence tells us what or whom we are talking about. The **predicate** tells us something about the subject.

Look at this sentence.

Koyo saw a robed figure.

To find out what the subject of the sentence is, we use ask the question, 'Who saw a robed figure?' The answer, 'Koyo', is the subject.

The rest of the sentence, including the verb, is the **predicate**.

A. Underline the subjects and circle the predicates.

1. The little dog barked when it saw the bone.
2. The bee stung the tired traveller.
3. My classroom is airy and clean.
4. The sun shines brightly.
5. The soldiers fought bravely in the battle.
6. I always say a prayer before I go to sleep.

B. Complete the sentences with suitable subjects or predicates.

1. The telephone ______________________.
2. ______________________ threw empty wrappers on the beach.
3. ______________________ are very pretty.
4. The giraffe ______________________.
5. Ravi and his brother ______________________.
6. The hungry tiger ______________________.

Word Forms: Verbs to Nouns

Many verbs have a related noun form.

Examples: Guno will **arrive** today. (verb)
I am waiting for Guno's **arrival**. (noun)

C. Write the noun forms of the following verbs.

1. entertain: ____________
2. act: ____________
3. behave: ____________
4. invite: ____________
5. laugh: ____________
6. refuse: ____________
7. think: ____________
8. grow: ____________
9. permit: ____________
10. know: ____________

Punctuation: Inverted commas

Read the sentences.

'Quick! Jump in,' said Guno.

'Oh, it is grand!' he exclaimed.

'Why don't you say something?' asked Koyo.

In these sentences, the exact words of the speakers are placed inside **inverted commas**.

In the first sentence, the comma is placed before a closed inverted comma.

In the second and third sentences, the exclamation mark and the question mark are also placed before a closed inverted comma.

The punctuation mark used with the exact words of the speaker always comes within inverted commas. Sentences within inverted commas always begin with a capital letter.

D. Rewrite these sentences after adding inverted commas in the correct places. You may have to add question marks and exclamation marks.

1. Guno said I am going to rob the Hadji's house.
2. My brother asked Can you see the baby elephant.
3. Going under water during scuba diving is the best experience I have ever had, Larry said.
4. Rajiv said How beautiful the flower is.
5. Are you sure they are not too heavy asked Rudy.
6. The children cried Look Lenny is flying.

Study Skills

Use Your Dictionary

Headwords are words at the top of the page in a dictionary. They indicate the first and the last words on the page.

Look at this page from a dictionary and write down the headwords.

Then, cover the page. Which of the following words appear on the page? Write 'Yes' or 'No' for each and check your answers once the task is complete.

1. haircut: ________
2. happy: ________
3. hall: ________
4. hamster: ________
5. handy: ________
6. hamper: ________
7. halfway: ________
8. handcuff: ________
9. halt: ________
10. hare: ________

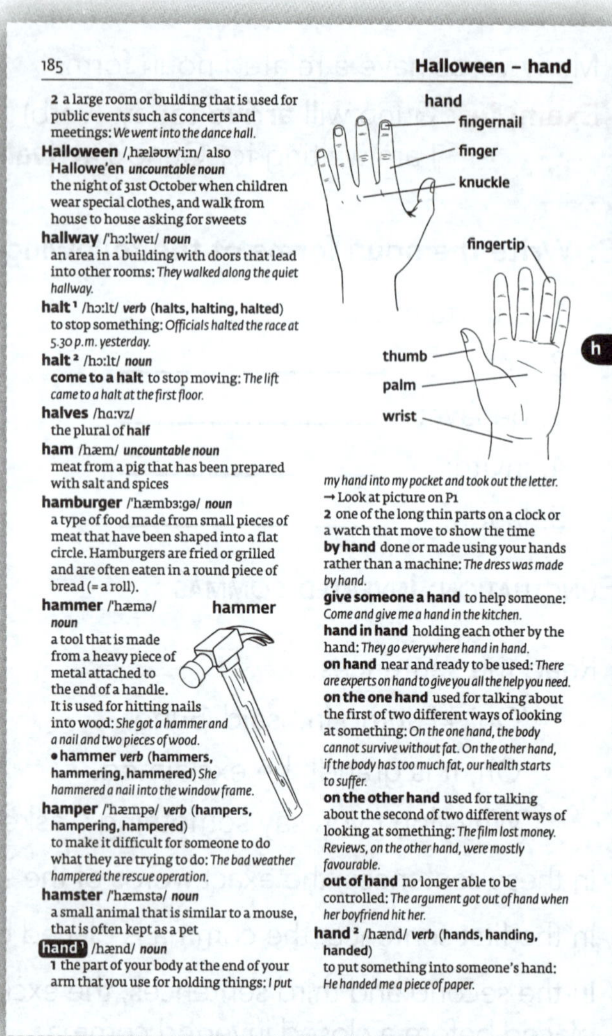

185 **Halloween – hand**

2 a large room or building that is used for public events such as concerts and meetings: *We went into the dance hall.*

Halloween /ˌhæləʊˈwiːn/ also **Hallowe'en** *uncountable noun* the night of 31st October when children wear special clothes, and walk from house to house asking for sweets

hallway /ˈhɔːlweɪ/ *noun* an area in a building with doors that lead into other rooms: *They walked along the quiet hallway.*

halt¹ /hɔːlt/ *verb* (**halts, halting, halted**) to stop something: *Officials halted the race at 5.30 p.m. yesterday.*

halt² /hɔːlt/ *noun* **come to a halt** to stop moving: *The lift came to a halt at the first floor.*

halves /hɑːvz/ the plural of **half**

ham /hæm/ *uncountable noun* meat from a pig that has been prepared with salt and spices

hamburger /ˈhæmbɜːɡə/ *noun* a type of food made from small pieces of meat that have been shaped into a flat circle. Hamburgers are fried or grilled and are often eaten in a round piece of bread (= a roll).

hammer /ˈhæmə/ *noun* a tool that is made from a heavy piece of metal attached to the end of a handle. It is used for hitting nails into wood: *She got a hammer and a nail and two pieces of wood.* • **hammer** *verb* (**hammers, hammering, hammered**) *She hammered a nail into the window frame.*

hamper /ˈhæmpə/ *verb* (**hampers, hampering, hampered**) to make it difficult for someone to do what they are trying to do: *The bad weather hampered the rescue operation.*

hamster /ˈhæmstə/ *noun* a small animal that is similar to a mouse, that is often kept as a pet

hand¹ /hænd/ *noun* **1** the part of your body at the end of your arm that you use for holding things: *I put my hand into my pocket and took out the letter.* → Look at picture on P1 **2** one of the long thin parts on a clock or a watch that move to show the time **by hand** done or made using your hands rather than a machine: *The dress was made by hand.* **give someone a hand** to help someone: *Come and give me a hand in the kitchen.* **hand in hand** holding each other by the hand: *They go everywhere hand in hand.* **on hand** near and ready to be used: *There are experts on hand to give you all the help you need.* **on the one hand** used for talking about the first of two different ways of looking at something: *On the one hand, the body cannot survive without fat. On the other hand, if the body has too much fat, our health starts to suffer.* **on the other hand** used for talking about the second of two different ways of looking at something: *The film lost money. Reviews, on the other hand, were mostly favourable.* **out of hand** no longer able to be controlled: *The argument got out of hand when her boyfriend hit her.*

hand² /hænd/ *verb* (**hands, handing, handed**) to put something into someone's hand: *He handed me a piece of paper.*

Listening and Speaking

Imagine that you and your friends are the villagers who caught Guno and Koyo. Form groups of five. The members of each group discuss and try to decide whether the thieves should be punished or allowed to go free. Take turns to conduct the discussion in class. Each group comes to a decision and shares the reasons for their choice with the rest of the class.

You can include the following points in your discussion:

- the crime committed by the thieves
- the place and the condition in which they were found
- what the villagers had wanted to do earlier

Pen it Down

Imagine that you are one of the villagers who found Guno and Koyo 'swimming' on the dry riverbed. Write a diary entry about what you learned after the thieves were caught and made to narrate what had happened. Try to make your entry funny.

You can include the following points in your entry:

- who the two tried to rob
- how they planned to escape
- who caught them and what the outcome was

HC **Feelings:** Participation in neighbourhood

Self Assessment

Now I can

- read and understand a story about two foolish thieves.
- practise phrasal verbs, transform a verb into a noun, identify subject and predicate and use punctuation correctly.
- participate in a group discussion and make a diary entry.

Read More

Folktales from India: This collection of tales by A. K. Ramanujan brings together fascinating stories from twenty-two different Indian languages.

Russian Fairy Tales: This is the most popular collection of Russian fairy tales, including the famous 'Firebird' and the 'Grey Wolf' stories. Put together by Alexander Afanasyev, the collection includes beautiful illustrations by Ivan Bilbin, inspired by Russian folk art.

5 Bread Making

E. L. M. King

SUSTAINABLE DEVELOPMENT GOALS 2 ZERO HUNGER

Let's Get Started

The United Nations Sustainable Development Goal 2 is about zero hunger. It states that we must ensure people have enough food and good nutrition. It also encourages people to try good farming practices.

Does your family bake bread or cake, or make rotis at home? Find nine words related to baking in the word grid and circle them.

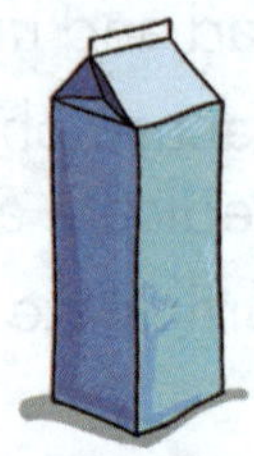

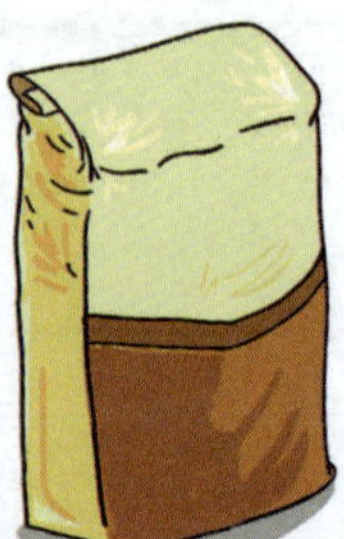

T	E	W	Q	C	V	C	T	P	O
O	B	U	T	T	E	R	W	L	I
X	D	Y	G	I	L	E	G	G	S
F	L	O	U	R	V	A	I	R	U
R	O	V	M	Q	X	M	Y	O	G
U	B	E	W	Z	Z	B	S	Q	A
I	L	N	U	T	S	M	A	Z	R
T	J	A	X	D	V	J	L	K	W
V	W	E	G	H	K	P	T	D	C
A	M	C	Y	I	M	I	L	K	V

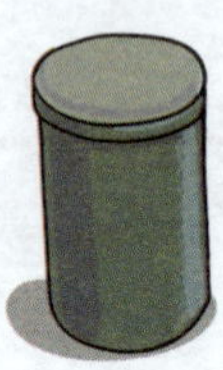

Active Participation: Joy of participation in family

Reading

Do you look forward to a particular food item being cooked at home? Do you offer to help when it is cooked? Read this poem about a child describing baking at home.

Mother's **kneading,** kneading **dough,**
In and out her **knuckles** go;
Till the sticky, shapeless lump
Grows a pillow, smooth and **plump**.

Then she cuts it, pops it in
To the neatly buttered tin,
Leaves it rising high and higher,
While she goes to make the fire.

How the glad flames leap and roar,
Through the open oven door;
Till their hot breath, as they play,[1]
Makes us wink and run away.

When they've burnt to **embers** red
Mother **shovels** in the bread;
And that warm, delicious smell
Tells her it is baking well.

When it's golden, just like wheat,
We shall get a **crust** to eat;
How I wish we could be fed
Every day on new-made bread!

kneading: pressing with the hands

dough: a thick mixture of flour and a liquid like water or milk

knuckles: the part where fingers join the hand

plump: well rounded

embers: small pieces of burning coal

shovels: places something with a shovel, a tool with a long handle and a blade

crust: slice of bread from the end of a loaf

Literary term

1. This is an example of **personification**. The flames are imagined as children who are breathing out as they play.

Who is kneading the dough?

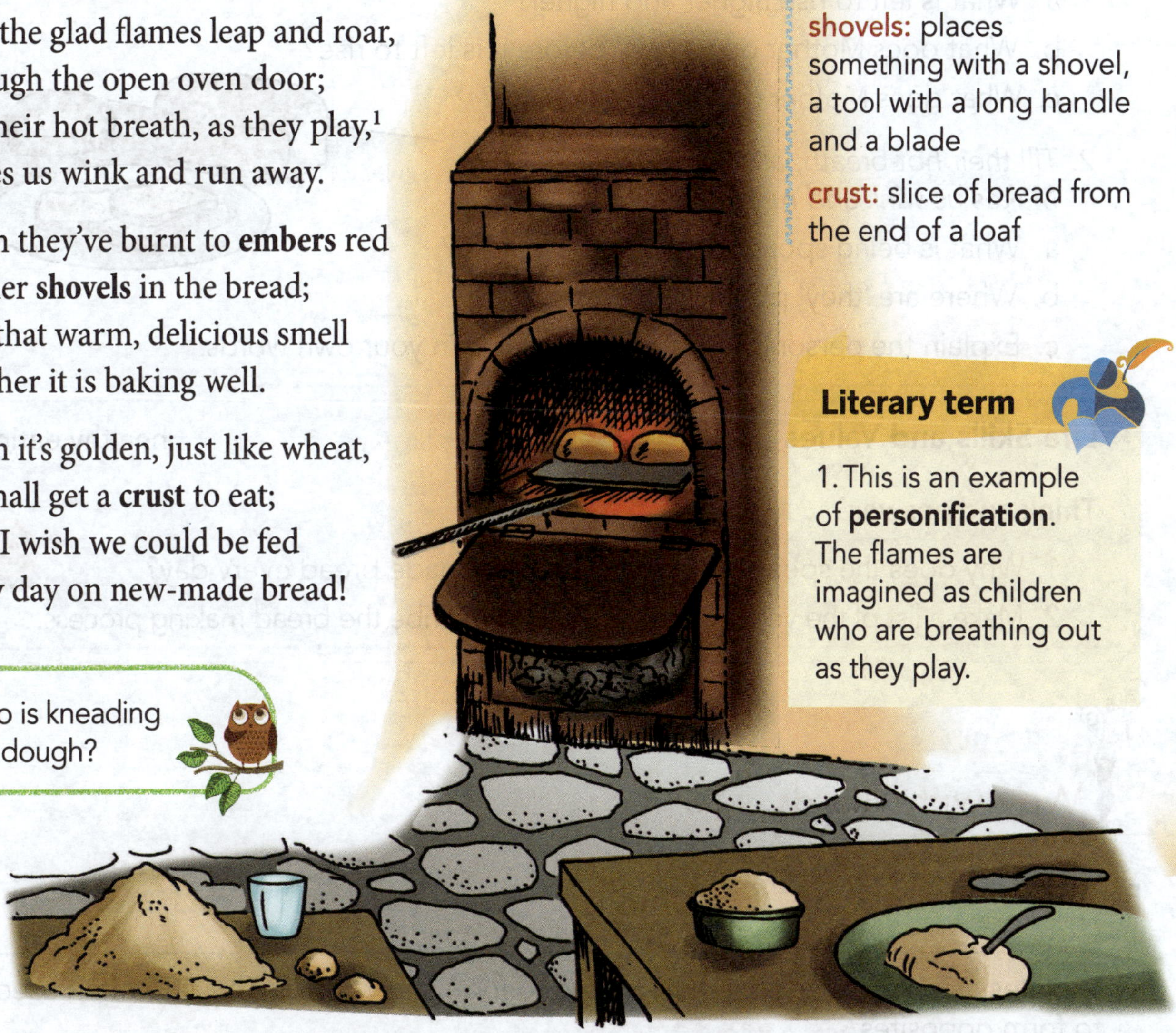

Comprehension

Quick Recap

A. Answer the questions in a few lines.

1. What was Mother doing? How did she knead the dough?
2. What is the meaning of the line, 'Till the sticky, shapeless lump/Grows a pillow...'?
3. Why did the children run away from the kitchen?
4. When did Mother shovel in the bread?
5. What told Mother that the bread was baking well?
6. When would the children get to eat the bread?

B. Read the lines from the poem and answer the questions.

1. *Leaves it rising high and higher*
   a. What is left to rise higher and higher?
   b. What does Mother do with 'it' before it is left to rise?
   c. What does Mother do in the meantime?

2. *Till their hot breath, as they play,*
   Makes us wink and run away.
   a. What is being spoken about in these lines?
   b. Where are 'they' playing?
   c. Explain the personification in the first line in your own words.

Life Skills and Values — healthy eating

Think and answer.

1. Why does the speaker wish to eat freshly made bread every day?
2. Make a list of the verbs the poet uses to describe the bread making process.

Way with Words

PREFIXES

Prefixes are letters added before a word to form a new word. They are often used to form opposites.

Some common prefixes are *un-*, *dis-* and *re-*.

Examples: belief → **dis**belief
fed → **un**fed
open → **re**open

A. Some of these words use the prefix dis- to form opposites. Underline the words and write their opposites.

appear	agree	danger	like	happy	comfort
mobile	blink	respect	help	return	believe

B. Complete the sentences using words formed by adding the prefixes un-, dis- or re- to the words in the brackets.

1. Sita does not exercise. She is very __________. (fit)
2. Rehan is __________ because his grandad has gone to his uncle's house in another city. (happy)
3. The tiger __________ when it heard the sound of footsteps. (appeared)
4. My new shoes are __________. (comfortable)
5. Mr Lal had to __________ Rs 5,000, which he had borrowed, to his friend. (pay)

C. Write five words that rhyme with tin. They can be of three or more letters.

1. ________ 2. ________ 3. ________ 4. ________ 5. ________

Grammar in Use

Simple Present Tense and Present Continuous Tense

Look at the sentence.

Then she **cuts** it, **pops** it in.

In this sentence, the verbs **cuts** and **pops** are in the simple present tense as they indicate actions which happen *now*.

The **simple present tense** is usually used to state a fact or talk about an action that happens on a regular basis.

Now, read this sentence.

Mother **is kneading** the dough.

Here, the verb **is kneading** is in the present continuous tense as it refers to an action which is happening now.

The **present continuous tense** tells us about an action that is going on at the time of speaking.

A. Complete the sentences using the simple present tense of the given verbs.

1. The teacher __________ her students to reach their goals. (inspire)
2. Ram __________ his teeth twice a day. (brush)
3. The children __________ television every evening. (watch)
4. My mother __________ to the market every Sunday. (go)
5. The Earth __________ round the Sun. (revolve)
6. Every night, I __________ a book before I go to sleep. (read)

B. Complete the sentences with the correct form of the given verbs.

1. Rima __________ football every day. (is playing/plays)
2. Vandana Katariya __________ (plays/is playing) for the Indian women's hockey team.
3. We __________ (study/are studying) science in our online class today.
4. My mother __________ (comes/is coming) home from work at 5 p.m.
5. My uncle has a weak knee. So, he __________ slowly. (is walking/walks)
6. I __________ my science project now. (am completing/completed)
7. Raja __________ to play the guitar. (is learning/learns)

Study Skills

Spell Check

The following words end in -sion, -cian or -tion. Some of them are spelt incorrectly. Identify them and write their correct spellings.

1. sesion	__________	5. admision	__________
2. action	__________	6. relasion	__________
3. decision	__________	7. condittion	__________
4. mucision	__________	8. electrition	__________

Listening and Speaking

Listen to a passage from Lewis Carroll's *Alice's Adventures in Wonderland* and answer the questions.

1. Where was Alice sitting?

2. What was her sister doing?
3. Why didn't Alice like the book she peeped into?
4. What was Alice planning to make?
5. Who ran past Alice?

Pen it Down

Work in pairs and create your own recipe for a refreshing summer drink. Write down the recipe, mentioning the following details:

- the ingredients and utensils that you need
- how to make the drink
- the time taken to prepare it and the number of people it serves

Self Assessment

Now I can

- read and understand a poem about how bread is made.
- practise prefixes, note down rhyming words, and use the simple present and present continuous tenses.
- write the correct spelling of words, and listen to a passage and answer questions.
- write a recipe, noting down the steps systematically.

Read More

The Toughest Pastry Maker: This funny poem by Kenn Nesbitt is about a boy who bakes cakes that no one can bite into, because he uses glue instead of milk or water.

All You Can Eat: This poem by Bruce Lansky describes what happens when the narrator goes to an eatery where one can eat as much as one wants.

6

Our Country

Rainmaking

Shankar

Let's Get Started

Do you enjoy the rains during monsoons? The monsoon season is very important for crops in India. If the monsoons are late, crops are affected and the price of goods goes up.

Complete the following information related to the monsoons. You can take the help of your teacher.

1. the months that form the monsoon season in your state:
2. the Indian state where the monsoons strike first:
3. the name of the monsoon season in your mother tongue:
4. an interesting memory of yours associated with the monsoons:

HC **Feelings:** Contributions in relationships (grandparents)

Reading

This passage is taken from the book,* Life with Grandfather, *which talks about a boy's experiences while living with his grandparents. Here, he remembers an evening when he got his grandfather wet by 'creating rain'. What do you think Grandfather said to him?

It was an evening after heavy rain. Grandfather was picking flowers from the jasmine bush under a sandalwood tree. The leaves of the tree were full of raindrops. I knew I could make rain if I shook the tree, and Grandfather and I would get a good shower. I liked bathing in the rain. Grandfather might not like it. But it would be great fun.

So I quietly went near the sandalwood tree and shook it with all my strength. There was a heavy shower and both Grandfather and I were soaked. I loved it. But Grandfather did not. He turned around with an angry look. I was sure he would catch me and beat me. So I ran. He ran after me. I ran fast. But he ran faster. He had almost caught me when he **stumbled** and fell. I ran away to the **paddy fields** and hid there. I heard Grandfather shout that he would teach me a lesson when I came back home.

Which tree did Raja shake to make rain?

I did not want to go home because I feared Grandfather would beat me. I stayed on in the fields. It was getting dark. I was afraid to stay there alone in the darkness. I remembered all the ghost stories I had heard. I stood up, looked around and then ran towards home.

I was still afraid of facing Grandfather. So I did not go into the house. I went to the cowshed and took shelter in the **loft**. From there I could see Grandfather sitting on the verandah, saying his prayers.

Grandmother was waiting for me. When I did not turn up, she looked for me everywhere in the house. Then, she came out and called me, thinking that I was somewhere in the garden. She did not get an answer. Then, she went to Grandfather and asked where I was. 'Look for him in the house,' Grandfather said. 'He is hiding somewhere.'

'He is not in the house,' Grandmother said. 'I looked for him everywhere.'

Then Grandfather stood up and went outside and called aloud, 'Come, Raja, come. I won't beat you.' But I did not answer him because I still thought he would beat me.

Did You Know? G.K.

The wood of the sandalwood tree is very valuable and is used to make perfumed oil and showpieces. It has a beautiful smell which lasts for many years. Sandalwood paste is used for religious ceremonies.

stumbled: lost balance

paddy fields: fields in which rice is grown

loft: a room under the roof, sometimes used for storing things

Why was Raja afraid of staying alone in the field?

courtyard: an open space in large houses, which is surrounded by buildings or walls

sympathies: showing that you understand and care about someone's problems

wailing: crying loudly

Why did Grandfather call the servants?

Grandmother was angry and said, 'He won't come. You drove him away. I heard you say that you would beat him if he came home. Poor child, he is afraid of you and has run away.'

Grandfather called the servants and asked them to go out and look for me. After a while, they too returned to say that they could not find me. Grandmother started weeping. Grandfather was walking up and down the **courtyard**.

The news that I was missing spread. Our neighbours came first, then our relatives and then, others who had heard the news. Many came to offer their **sympathies** to Grandmother. Grandfather did not like this. He shouted, 'Nothing has happened to the boy! He is hiding somewhere. Can't some of you go out and find him instead of wasting your time here?'

Some of them went out to search for me. More and more people came and soon there was a crowd. By now Grandmother had lost all hope of seeing me again. She started telling the people what a good boy I was.

The search parties returned without finding me. Grandmother started weeping loudly. The women in the crowd also wept. The servants of the house joined in the **wailing**. They all acted as if I were dead.

I felt very sorry for Grandmother. I wanted to come out. Grandfather was a man of strong will. But I knew that he too felt very sad. However, he did not lose hope. He stood up, turned in the direction of our family temple and prayed. 'Help me, God,' he said. 'Give me my child. I want him now. I cannot wait.' He then stood silent in prayer.

At that moment, my uncle returned. He learnt what was happening at home. He looked around and guessed where I was. He came to the cowshed and asked me to come down. When I came down, he took me into the house.

How did the people react when Raja went missing?

Grandfather had just finished his prayer. As he opened his eyes, he saw me standing before him. He took me up in his arms in joy, hugged me and said, 'God heard my prayers and has given you back to us.'

What did Grandfather say after Raja was found?

About the author

Shankar, or K. Shankar Pillai (1902–1989), was a well-known Indian cartoonist. He is considered the father of political cartooning in India. He founded the Children's Book Trust, which publishes books for children.

Comprehension

Quick Recap

A. Answer the questions in a few lines.

1. What was Grandfather doing in the garden?
2. How did Raja 'create' rain?
3. Why did Raja run away from Grandfather?
4. Where did he run and hide?
5. What did Raja do after returning from the fields?
6. Why was Grandmother angry with Grandfather?
7. What news spread among the neighbours? Why did everyone start crying?
8. Who finally found Raja? How did he bring the boy back to the house?

B. Read the lines from the story and answer the questions.

1. *She started telling everyone what a good boy I was.*
   a. Who is referred to as 'she'?
   b. Who was she speaking about?
   c. Why was she telling everyone that 'he' was a 'good boy'?
2. *'I want him now. I cannot wait.'*
   a. Who said these words and to whom?
   b. Why could the speaker not wait any longer?
   c. What happened after the speaker said these words?

Life Skills and Values

honesty, responsibility

Think and answer.

1. What could Raja have done instead of hiding and making everyone worry about him?
2. What kind of a person was Raja's grandfather? How was he different from Grandmother?

Way with Words

Contextual Usage

A. Complete the sentences with words from the box. Note that there are more words than the blanks.

quietly	soaked	strength	shelter	stumbled
weeping	fields	will	prayer	hiding

1. When Rani couldn't find her doll, she started ________________.
2. The thief was ________________ behind the curtain.
3. My father is a man of strong ________________. He always does what he thinks is right.
4. We should say a ________________ before our meal.
5. Harsh was sure to come first in the race, but he ________________ and fell.
6. Suddenly, it started raining heavily and all of us were ________________ to the skin.
7. We took ________________ in the neighbour's verandah when the storm began.

Analogies

When we draw an **analogy** between two things, we compare them because they are alike in some way.

Example: calf is to **cow** as cub is to **lion**

B. Complete these word pairs. The first one is done for you.

1. *doctor is to hospital as teacher is to school*
2. pen is to author as brush is to ________________
3. comb is to hair as toothbrush is to ________________
4. egg is to chicken as milk is to ________________
5. dog is to kennel as horse is to ________________

Grammar in Use

Adjectives: Degrees of Comparison

You know that adjectives can be used in the **positive, comparative** and **superlative** degrees.

The comparative and the superlative degrees are usually formed by adding **-er** and **-est**, respectively, to the adjective.

Examples: My uncle had an **angry** look on his face. (positive)
My grandmother had an **angrier** look than my uncle. (comparative)
My grandfather had the **angriest** look of them all. (superlative)

But in some adjectives, we add the words **more** and **most** to form the comparative and superlative degrees.

Examples: Raja's uncle was **intelligent**.
Raja's grandmother was **more intelligent**.
Raja's grandfather was **most intelligent**.

Some adjectives change completely in the comparative and superlative degrees. The spelling changes completely from the positive to the comparative and superlative degrees.

positive	comparative	superlative
good	better	best
bad	worse	worst
many	more	most

A. Complete the sentences with the correct degree of comparison of the adjectives.

1. My father is tall. My uncle is ______________ than my father.
2. The math test was easy, but the science test was the ______________.
3. Florida is ______________. Do you know the sunniest place in the USA?
4. Kapil is a successful sportsman, but his sister is ______________ than Kapil.
5. My mother has a soft voice, but my teacher's voice is ______________ than my mother's.
6. Delhi is cold in winter but Manali is ______________ than Delhi.

Word Forms: Verbs and Nouns

We use many words both as nouns and as verbs.

Examples: We must drink plenty of **water** to remain healthy. (noun)
I **water** the plants in the garden every day. (verb)

B. Fill in the blanks with the words from the help box as nouns and verbs. Then write N for noun and V for verb.

search rain play watch

1. I ______________ the news every day.
My parents bought me a new ______________ on my birthday.

2. Jessie will act in the school _______________ this year.
   Ross will _______________ one of the elves in *The Elves and the Shoemaker.*
3. The weather report says that it will _______________ heavily throughout the weekend.
   The sudden _______________ wet the clothes on the balcony.
4. The _______________ for the queen's missing diamond went on for a week.
   Radha will _______________ for her missing dog in her colony.

Study Skills

Use Your Dictionary

Write three words that mean the same as these words. Use a dictionary if required.

1. child _______________ _______________ _______________
2. angry _______________ _______________ _______________
3. wailing _______________ _______________ _______________
4. afraid _______________ _______________ _______________
5. sad _______________ _______________ _______________

Listening and Speaking

Listen to a passage about Arif's gift to his mother on Mother's Day. The, discuss the importance of parents in your life and talk about how you can show them that you love them.

You can include these points:

- by obeying your parents
- by helping in household chores
- by making a handmade gift on a special occasion for them

Pen it Down

A. Make a list of five things that you enjoy doing with your grandparents and write why you like doing them.

B. Imagine that you are Raja. Write a note to your grandparents saying that you are sorry for what you did. You should explain why you hid in the loft and mention that you are sorry for making them worried.

Self Assessment

Now I can

- read about the special bond between grandparents and grandchildren.
- practise analogies, degrees of comparison of adjectives and use words as both nouns and verbs.
- discuss a given topic in class, make a list and write a note to my grandparents.

Read More

Tiger in the House: This story by Ruskin Bond is about a boy's experiences with a tiger cub his grandfather brought home from a hunting trip.

Fablehaven: This book by Brandon Mull is about the adventures of Kendra and her brother, Seth, who discover during their holidays that their grandparents' home is a protected area for magical creatures, witches and trolls. And their grandfather is the caretaker!

Be Creative!

A. In 'Guno and Koyo', you read about a foolish thief who tries to steal a beautiful robe. Design an item of clothing for yourself, with one magical feature. Give a name to the dress like 'Flying Shirt', draw it and write about its magical quality.

Name: ______________________________

B. 1. Circle all the words in the box that are synonyms of the word 'good'.

perfect	dreadful	decide	superior	superb
correct	strong	excellent	welcome	marvellous
select	minor	wonderful	principal	fun

2. Make sentences with any of the three synonyms.

C. In 'Rainmaking', you read about a boy's experience of living with his grandparents. Now, read the following paragraph and complete the story in ten sentences.

Kamal was visiting his grandparents' house in the village during his winter vacation. After a few days, he was bored because he had nothing to do. School would reopen ten days later. So, he decided to explore the attic of the house. He climbed up and before he entered the attic, he noticed a door to his left. He was surprised because he had never seen it before. He went in and saw a large box in the middle of the room...

poem: rap

7

The Recycling Rap

John Foster

Let's Get Started

The United Nations Sustainable Development Goal 12 is about using things responsibly. It promotes using the Earth's resources without harming Nature, producing less waste and recycling waste goods instead of letting them end up in landfills.

Complete this recycling activity. Look at the given words. Sort the trash by placing recyclable items in the green bucket and the non-recyclable items in the red bucket.

used paper	old batteries	torn clothes	newspapers
vegetable scraps	plastic bottles	expired medicines	old markers

Active Participation: Joy of participation in the collective

Reading

What do you do with empty bottles, old newspapers, wrappers and packing materials after using them? People often throw these things away without much thought. Read

recycling: making new things out of old products

reclamation: getting materials from waste products so that they can be reused

sitting on the fence: not taking a decision about something

claptrap: foolish talk

rap: a type of popular music with a strong rhythm and fast spoken words

tip: (American English) a garbage dump

skip: a large open container for waste

bottle bank: a large container in a public place where people can leave bottles for recycling

squash: press and flatten something

Save-A-Can: an organisation which collects empty cans and recycles them

Name two recyclable items.

Did You Know? Science

An average person generates about 1.5 kg of rubbish each day. Germany, Slovenia and Austria recycle more than 60 per cent of their waste.

this poem about the importance of recycling things.

Listen to me, children. Hear what I say.
We've got to start **recycling**. It's the only way
To save this planet for future generations—
The name of the game is **reclamation**.
You've got to start recycling. You know it makes sense.
You've got to start recycling. Stop **sitting on the fence**.
No more waiting. No more **claptrap**.
Get yourself doing the recycling **rap**.

Come on and start recycling. Start today
By saving old newspapers, not throwing them away,
Don't just take them and dump them on the **tip**,
Tie them in a bundle and put them in the **skip**.

Get collecting, protecting the future's up to you.
Save all your old glass bottles and your jam jars too.
Take them to the **bottle bank**, then at the factory
The glass can be recycled, saving energy.

Don't throw away that empty drink can.
Remember what I said. Start recycling, man.
Wash it, **squash** it, squeeze it flat and thin.
Take it to the **Save-A-Can** and post it in.

Listen to me, children. Hear what I say.
We've got to start recycling. It's the only way
To save this planet for future generations—
The name of the game is reclamation.

You've got to start recycling. You know it makes sense.
You've got to start recycling. Stop sitting on the fence.
No more **pussyfooting**. No more claptrap.
Get yourself doing the recycling rap.

pussyfooting: (informal) the act of behaving in an excessively cautious way by avoiding the issue

About the poet

John Foster (1941–) is a former teacher and a children's poet in the UK. He has written twelve books of poetry for children, and likes to perform his poems on visits to schools.

Comprehension

Quick Recap

A. Answer the questions in a few lines.

1. What is the meaning of the phrase, 'sitting on the fence'?
2. What does the speaker want children to do?
3. How can newspapers be recycled?
4. What should children do with old glass bottles and jam jars?

B. Read the lines from the poem and answer the questions.

1. *It's the only way*
   To save this planet for future generations—
   a. What is the only way to save the planet?
   b. Who should the planet be saved for?
   c. What, according to the speaker, is the 'name of the game'?
2. *Wash it, squash it, squeeze it flat and thin.*
   a. What does 'it' refer to?
   b. Why does the speaker want 'it' to be washed, squashed and squeezed flat?
   c. Where does the speaker want 'it' to be taken?

Life Skills and Values — saving the environment

Think and answer.

1. The poet repeats a number of lines in the poem. What effect does repetition create in the poem?
2. Make a list of the items which can be recycled. Where can they be taken for recycling?

Way with Words

Word Pairs

Word pairs are words which are commonly used together and joined by **and/or**.
Examples: give and take, wait and see, right or wrong

Match the following to form suitable word pairs. Then, make sentences with them.

A		B
1. bed	and	a. forth
2. work		b. wide
3. bits		c. pieces
4. back		d. play
5. far		e. breakfast
6. salt		f. pepper

Grammar in Use

Possessive Adjectives and Possessive Pronouns

Look at the sentence.

This is **my** jam jar.

Here, the word **my** is a possessive adjective.

Possessive adjectives show to whom something belongs and are used before nouns.

The sentence can also be written as: The jam jar is **mine**.

Here, **mine** is a possessive pronoun.

A **possessive pronoun** is used in place of a noun, to show belonging.

A. Complete these sentences with either possessive adjectives or possessive pronouns.

1. Is that ______________ bag? (your/yours)
2. The last slice of the cake is ______________. (your/yours)
3. That bag is ______________. (my/mine)
4. That is ______________ bag. (my/mine)
5. ______________ car is white. (Her/Hers)

Main and Auxiliary Verbs

The **main verb** in a sentence denotes the action of the subject and can stand alone. It can also be used with a helping verb, which is referred to as an **auxiliary verb**.

Examples:

You've got to start recycling. (*you have*)

In the sentence, **you've** is a contracted form of **you** + **have**, while **got** is the main verb and **have** is the auxiliary verb.

The auxiliary verbs **be**, **do** and **have** take the forms given in the table.

Present tense (Singular/Plural)	Past tense (Singular/Plural)
is/are/am	was/were
does/do	did
has/have	had

B. Fill in the blanks with suitable auxiliary verbs.

1. The carpenters ______________ completed their work.
2. What ______________ the students doing when the teacher entered the classroom?
3. I ______________ going to watch a film with my friends.
4. What ______________ she do in the afternoon on weekdays?
5. The boy ______________ cleaning his room.
6. ______________ he help you clean the house?

Study Skills

Spell Check

The spellings of words ending in **-ar** and **-er** are often confused because the letters are pronounced in the same way.

Complete the words by adding -ar or -er.

coll____	gramm____	hamm____	pill____	nect____	form____
prison____	farm____	lawy____	mill____	begg____	fath____

Listening and Speaking

A. Listen to the passage and arrange these sentences in the correct sequence.

- ☐ I jumped out of bed.
- ☐ I had a good day in school.
- ☐ Mother was standing with a toothbrush in one hand.
- ☐ I was dreaming that I was a superhero.
- ☐ I was eager to get home and sleep.
- ☐ Mother said that she would not allow me to go to the party.

Pen it Down

A notice is used to announce or display information. It is generally put up on display boards in schools and in public places. It includes:

- the title 'NOTICE' and date.
- the name of the institute/office putting up the notice.
- a heading to introduce the subject of the notice.
- the body of the notice, with important details.
- the writer's signature, name and designation (if any) in block letters.

NOTICE

Name of the institution

Heading

Date

[Body of the notice] ______________________

____

____

____

Signature

Name

Designation

Your school is organising a 'Recycle and Reuse' camp with a voluntary organisation, in which students would be taught to make useful things out of waste materials. Write a notice requesting students to participate in the camp. Give information about the event, including the date, time and venue.

Self Assessment

Now I can

- read and understand a poem about recycling and reducing waste.
- recognize word pairs and practise using main and auxiliary verbs, and possessive adjectives and possessive pronouns.
- spell words with -ar and -er, speak on a given topic and write a notice accurately.

Read More

Write a Rap: This poem by John Foster is about how to write a 'rap' poem using rhyming words.

You Can't Be That: This poem by Brian Patten is about what a little child really wants to be when he grows up.

8

A Crow in the House

Ruskin Bond

Let's Get Started

Complete the following details to find out how well you know the people in your neighbourhood.

1. The oldest person in your neighbourhood and their age:
2. A person in your neighbourhood who is usually very helpful:
3. A helpful initiative in your neighbourhood. Whom is it for?
4. Two rules in your neighbourhood which everyone has to follow:

HC **Learning and Awareness:** Coexistence in society and nature

Reading

Have you ever taken care of an injured animal or bird? In this story, a boy comes across an injured crow and decides to take care of it. Find out what happens after the crow recovers.

A young crow had fallen from its nest and was **fluttering** about on the road, in danger of being crushed by a car or a *tonga*, or being **seized** by a cat, before I brought it home. It was in a sorry state, beak **gaping** and head **drooping**. We did not expect it to **survive**. But my Grandfather and I did our best to bring it around. We fed it by gently **prising** its beak open to allow it to swallow. The young crow was soon on its way to recovery.

fluttering: flapping (its) wings up and down
seized: caught
gaping: wide open
drooping: hanging
survive: live in spite of difficult events
prising: opening by force

Did You Know? ? **G.K.**

A *tonga* is a, two-wheeled vehicle, which is drawn by horses. It is used in India.

He was offered his freedom but did not take it. Instead he made himself at home in our house. My Grandfather, Aunt Mabel and even some of Grandfather's pets **objected** to it but there was no way we could get rid of the crow. The crow took over the **administration** of the house. We were not sure if it was a male, but we named it Caesar.

Soon, Caesar was joining us at mealtimes besides finding his own **grubs** or beetles in the garden. He danced about on the dining table and gave us no peace till he had been given his small bowl of meat, soup and vegetables. He was always **restless**, **fidgeting** about, **investigating** things. He would hop about a table to empty a matchbox of its contents, or rip the daily paper to shreds, overturn a vase of flowers or tug at the tail of one of the dogs. 'That crow will ruin us,' grumbled my Grandmother, picking marigolds off the carpet. 'Can't you keep him in a cage?'

We did try putting Caesar in a cage but he became so angry and objected with such fierce cawing and flapping that it was better for our nerves and peace of mind to give him the run of the house. He did not show any **inclination** to join the other crows in the banyan tree. Grandfather said this was because he was really a jungle crow—a raven of sorts and probably felt **contempt** towards ordinary crows. But it seemed to me that Caesar had grown so used to living with humans that he had become **snobbish** and did not wish to mix with his own kind. He would even **squabble** with Harold, the **hornbill**. Perching on top of Harold's cage, he would peck at the big bird's feet. Harold would scold him, and try to catch him through the bars.

In time, Caesar learned to talk a little, as ravens sometimes do, in a cracked, throaty voice. He would sit for hours outside the window, banging on the glass and calling 'Hello, hello.' He seemed to recognise the click of the gate when I came home from school and would come to the door with a hop, skip and a jump to say 'Hello, hello.' I had also taught him to sit on my arm and say, 'Kiss, kiss' while he placed his head gently against my mouth.

objected: showed dislike for

administration: running, management

grubs: larvae of an insect

restless: unable to be still

fidgeting: moving about restlessly

investigating: checking something closely to find out more about it

inclination: wish

contempt: disrespect

snobbish: feeling of being better than others

squabble: fight

hornbill: a bird with a long, curved beak

How did Caesar behave inside the cage?

On one of Aunt Mabel's visits, he came and sat on her arm and cackled, 'Kiss, kiss.' Aunt Mabel was delighted and probably flattered, and leant forward for a kiss. But Caesar's attention had shifted to my aunt's gleaming spectacles and poking at them with his beak, he knocked them off. Aunt Mabel was never a success with pets.

engaging: interesting, pleasant

spied: kept a close watch

fascinated: highly interested

disaster: something unexpected which harms a lot of people

helping himself to: stealing

antisocial: unfriendly

shallow: not deep

Grandmother insisted that Caesar was a pest in spite of his **engaging** habits. If he had only behaved this way in his own house, it would not have been so bad; but he took to visiting neighbours' houses and stealing pens and pencils, hair ribbons, combs, toys, shuttlecocks, toothbrushes and false teeth. He was especially fond of toothbrushes and made a collection of them on top of the cupboard in my room. Most of the neighbours were represented in our house by a toothbrush. Toothbrush sales went up that year and so did Grandmother's blood pressure.

What was Caesar especially fond of?

Caesar **spied** on children going to the *baniya's* shop and often managed to snatch sweets from them as they came out. Clothes pegs **fascinated** him. Neighbours would return from the bazaar to find their washing lying in the mud with no sign of the pegs. These pegs too found their way to the top of the cupboard.

It was Caesar's gardening activities which finally led to **disaster**. He was **helping himself to** a neighbour's beans when someone flung a stick at him, breaking his leg. I carried the bird home and both Grandfather and I washed and bandaged his leg as best as we could. But it would not mend. Caesar hung his head and no longer talked. He grew weaker day by day, refusing to eat.

Where was Caesar found dead?

One morning I found him dead on the sofa, his legs stiff in the air. Poor Caesar! His **antisocial** habits had led to his early end. I dug a **shallow** grave in the garden and buried him there along with all the toothbrushes and clothes pegs he had collected.

About the author

Ruskin Bond (1934–) is an Anglo-Indian author. He is best-known for his short stories set in Himalayan towns. Some of his most-loved stories are 'Harold the Hornbill' and 'Tiger in the Tunnel'.

Comprehension

Quick Recap

A. Answer the questions in a few lines.

1. In what condition did the narrator find the crow?
2. How did the narrator and his grandfather nurse the crow back to health?
3. What were some of the crow's daily activities at home?
4. According to the narrator, why did Caesar not mix with other crows?
5. What happened during Aunt Mabel's visit?
6. How did Caesar disturb the neighbours?
7. What led to Caesar's early end?
8. How did the narrator show his love for the crow?

B. Read the lines from the story and answer the questions.

1. *'That crow will ruin us.'*
   a. Who said these words? Why?
   b. What was the speaker doing while saying this?
   c. What did the speaker suggest doing with the crow?

2. *These pegs too found their way to the top of the cupboard.*
   a. Who brought the pegs to the top of the cupboard and from where?
   b. What happened because he took away the pegs?
   c. What else was on top of the cupboard?

Life Skills and Values caring for animals and birds, kindness

Think and answer.

1. Why do you think Caesar did not want to be kept in a cage?
2. How do we know that the crow developed a special liking for the narrator?
3. Why did the narrator call the crow's habits 'antisocial'?

Critical Thinking

Way with Words

Commonly Confused Words

A. Choose the correct word to complete the sentences.

1. John noted down the address of the nearest ________ in his pocket ________. (diary/dairy)
2. ________ is a table in the corner where the children can collect ________ prizes. (their/there)
3. The tyre ________ the cycle came ________. (of/off)
4. We were ________. So, we decided to play a ________ game. (board/bored)
5. Please come ________ because I can't ________ you. (hear/here)
6. I have to ________ a new pair of shoes ________ this weekend. (by/buy)

Contextual Usage

B. Complete the sentences with the following words from the story.

fierce	flattered	represented	stiff	occasional

1. The traveller was very thirsty, but he only had an ____________ sip of water so that it lasted the journey.
2. The Tasmanian Devil is a ____________ and short-tempered animal.
3. Can you buy some ____________ cardboard for the art project?
4. Sunita ____________ her school in the art competition.
5. The sly fox ____________ the foolish giraffe, saying that he was the bravest of all animals and should be made king.

Grammar in Use

Using *Who* and *Which*

Look at the sentences.

It was Caesar's gardening activities **which** finally led to disaster.

It was Grandfather **who** discovered the pegs on top of the cupboard.

We use **which** to refer to things and **who** to refer to people.

A. Join these sentences using who or which. You may have to make some necessary changes.

1. This is the boy. The boy brought home an injured crow.
2. This is the shop. The shop sells toy robots.
3. These are the footballers. They practise in the stadium every morning.
4. This is our new computer. My brother put it together.
5. This is a photo of Mother Teresa. She took care of the poor and the sick.
6. My aunt is a scientist. She studies plants.

Subject-Verb Agreement

Look at these sentences.

Aunt Mabel **was** delighted.

Here, the singular noun 'Aunt Mabel' is followed by the singular verb 'was'.

The children **have** to go to school on Sunday.

Here, the plural noun 'children' is followed by the plural verb 'have'. This is known as the agreement of the verb with the subject.

B. Complete the sentences with the correct verb.

1. Mother ___________ (has/have) to go to the market to buy vegetables.
2. The children ___________ (is/are) going to complete their work on time.
3. The teacher ___________ (has/have) to correct all the papers in an hour.
4. My friend ___________ (is/are) the captain of our cricket team.
5. Ravi and Rohan ___________ (has/have) to compete with each other to win the medal.
6. We ___________ (is/are) making a scrapbook as a birthday present for our friend.
7. All the students in the class ___________ (has/have) gone for a picnic.
8. The naughty boy ___________ (has/have) broken the beautiful vase.

Study Skills

STRESSED LETTERS IN A WORD

Pronounce Well

Listen to your teacher say the following words and repeat them. Listen carefully to the way he/she says them, putting force or stress at the beginning of each word.

pilot collar driver waiter dairy dentist

Now, listen to the following words. You will notice that the stress is at the end of the words. Repeat them carefully.

Japan unkind before upon around behind

Look at the following list of words. In some words, the stress is at the beginning and in some, the stress is at the end. Read them aloud and write them in the correct column. Then, add two words of your own to each column.

water begin people heating ahead because

stress at the beginning	stress at the end

Listening and Speaking

Listen to a passage about a mysterious stranger and answer the questions.

1. Where had the girl's parents gone?
2. What was the girl's sister doing?
3. Why did the girl rush to open the door?
4. Which adjective has been used to describe the man standing at the doorstep?
5. Describe what the man was wearing.

What would you do if you were in the same situation as the girl? Would you open the door to let the man in, or ask him to come back after your parents returned? Say five sentences on the topic in your own words.

Pen it Down

If you could have an imaginary animal for a pet, what kind of creature would it be? Write a paragraph describing it and draw a picture of it.

Remember to include the following details:

- what the pet would look like
- what it would eat
- how you would take care of it

Learning and Awareness: Recognizing characteristics and nature of entities

Self Assessment

Now I can

- read and understand a story about helping animals and caring for them.
- recognize commonly confused words, correctly use *who* and *which*, and understand subject-verb agreement.
- listen to a passage and answer questions, speak on a given topic and write a paragraph about an imaginary animal.

Read More

The Butterfly Lion: This book by Michael Morpurgo is about the love between an orphaned white lion cub and Bertie, a boy who rescues him from the African forest.

The Parrot Who Wouldn't Talk and Other Stories: This book by Ruskin Bond includes well-loved characters from other stories by the author, like Grandfather, the unusual Uncle Ken who often gets into trouble, and Aunt Ruby, whose parrot refuses to speak.

9 Life Cycle of a Butterfly

Rehana Ali

Let's Get Started

The United Nations Sustainable Development Goal 15 is about life on land. It says that we must try to protect our forests, and all plants, birds and animals that live in them.

Discuss the life cycle of a butterfly with your teacher and label the diagram. Use the words in the help box.

eggs	butterfly	larva	pupa

Learning and Awareness: Bodily activities and needs

Reading

Have you seen a caterpillar, with its body covered in tiny thorns? Did you ever wonder how the worm changes into a pretty insect like the butterfly?

Where was the caterpillar while she was dreaming?

tendrils: thread-like stems of climbing plants

cocoon: silky case which the larva makes

chrysalis: hard case in which the young insect lies before it reaches the adult stage

curvy: curly

slender: thin and graceful

feelers: long, wiry parts on the heads of insects

drape: cover

wriggle: twist and turn with quick movements

poised: all set; fixed in one place but ready to move at any moment

blur: a shape that can't be seen clearly

dainty: delicate; small and pretty

springs: gives

Read a poem about this change, called 'metamorphosis', which is one of the wonders of Nature.

A little caterpillar
Crunched and munched all day,
On **tendrils**, leaves and tiny buds
And all that came her way.

And when she was quite filled up
She just went off to sleep,
She wove a cosy **cocoon**
And slid into it deep.
And while this little larva
Was lost in her dream world,
A miracle was taking place
In the **chrysalis** where she lay curled.

Our little roly-poly friend
Was growing a **curvy** shape,
Slender legs and **feelers**
And beautiful wings to **drape**,

Her now slim and slender body,
Waited until the time was right,
For her to **wriggle** from the wrap
And face the daylight bright.

For just a tiny moment
She waited, **poised** to fly,
And when her beautiful wings had dried,
She sailed into the sky.

A **blur** of colour, warm and bright
A **dainty** rainbow drop,
She sang and danced all through the day
From flower to flower she hopped.

The happy little butterfly
Soon built a home again,
And on a leaf she laid her eggs
A new life thus began.

So, from a caterpillar
To a pretty butterfly,
Life **springs** its own surprises
But she keeps on flying high.

Did You Know? Science

A caterpillar grows so much that it gets too big for its skin and needs to shed its skin five or six times.

The butterfly's wings are transparent. They are made of thousands of layers, which reflect light in different colours.

About the poet

Rehana Ali is a teacher who lives and teaches in Lucknow.

Comprehension

Quick Recap

A. Answer the questions in a few lines.

1. What did the caterpillar eat?
2. What happened to the caterpillar inside the cocoon?
3. When did the butterfly get ready to fly?
4. What did the butterfly do all day?
5. How does the poet describe the butterfly?
6. What is referred to as the butterfly's home?

B. Read the lines from the poem and answer the questions.

1. *And when she was quite filled up*
   a. Who does 'she' refer to?
   b. What does the phrase 'filled up' mean?
   c. What did she do when she was filled up?
2. *For her to wriggle from the wrap*
   a. What does the 'wrap' refer to?
   b. What happened inside the wrap?
   c. What is she ready to do now?

Life Skills and Values understanding science

Think and answer.

1. Do you think the transformation of the caterpillar into a butterfly is a miracle? Why?
2. What do you understand by the statement, 'Life springs its own surprises'?

Way with Words

Jumbled Words

A. Rearrange the letters to form words related to butterflies.

1. gswni __________ 2. rvala __________ 3. nocooc __________
4. llcatarerpi __________ 5. elseefr __________ 6. ysalischr __________

Word Order in Sentences

The words in a sentence always have to follow a strict order so that they are grammatically correct and meaningful. Look at this sentence.

And when she was quite filled up, she just went off to sleep.

Now, look at this sentence.

And when she was filled quite up, she sleep off to went.

The sentence is no longer meaningful or grammatically correct.

B. Rearrange the order of words in these sentences to make them meaningful.

1. The teacher the asked student a question.
2. The butterfly changes into a larva.
3. What you did have for dinner?
4. I can borrow a book from the library?
5. The spear carried a sword and a soldier.
6. The old man saved the little girl drowning from.

Grammar in Use

Simple Future Tense

We use the **simple future tense** to talk about an action or event that hasn't yet started but will happen in the future.

The simple future tense is formed by adding **will** before the base form of a verb.

Examples: The insect **will munch** on leaves.
The caterpillar **will sleep** inside its cocoon.

A. Complete the following sentences with the future tense of the given verbs.

watch perform play post visit pick

1. My father ________________ us up from school tomorrow.
2. She ________________ the letter on her way to office.
3. I ________________ my grandparents over the weekend.
4. He ________________ at the show on Saturday.
5. Bina ________________ a film on her birthday.
6. We ________________ a cricket match on Monday.

Study Skills

Spell Check

Complete these words using -ent or -ant.

1. pleas________ 2. const________ 3. mom________ 4. abs________
5. rec________ 6. brilli________ 7. pres________ 8. intellig________

Listening and Speaking

When we speak, we say the nouns, verbs, adjectives and adverbs more forcefully, or with greater stress. We do not stress articles, prepositions and helping verbs.

A. Listen to these sentences and repeat them, with stress on the words in bold.

- **I** can **play** the **guitar.**
- **Raj** will **eat** a **sandwich** and **fries** for **lunch.**
- **We** will **go** for a **holiday** next **year.**

Now, say these sentences with the correct stress.

1. Joseph likes to play football in the evening.
2. Shabnam is singing a song in the Christmas concert.
3. Sethu studies for three hours every day.
4. Do you want some ice cream?

B. Do you know any poems on the butterfly? With the help of your partner, find a simple poem on the butterfly or any other creature and recite it in the next class.

Pen it Down

21ST CENTURY Creativity

Do you ever wonder what it would be like if you had wings and could fly? Write a paragraph beginning with 'If I had wings ...'.

You can include the following points:

- what you would do
- where you would go
- how you would feel

Self Assessment

Now I can

- read and understand a poem about the way a caterpillar changes into a butterfly.
- rearrange words into meaningful sentences and use the simple future tense.
- understand word stress in a sentence, recite a poem and write a paragraph on a given topic

10

Oliver Goes to London

Charles Dickens

Let's Get Started

Complete the passage using the given words and learn about the difficult conditions that poor children in 19th century England found themselves in. The story you will read in this chapter is set in the same time and place.

play	paid	hours	shoe polish	four	mines	parents

In the 19th century, small children often had to work for money. Children as young as ________ were forced to work in factories. When poor ________ couldn't return the money that they had borrowed from rich factory owners, their children were made to work to pay off their debts. They were not ________ well and were made to work in coal ________, cotton mills and as servants in people's homes. They had to work up to twelve ________ in very unhealthy conditions. They couldn't even take enough breaks to rest or ________! When the author Charles Dickens was 12 years old, he worked in a factory that made ________ ________. He wrote famous novels like *Oliver Twist* and *David Copperfield*, which described the conditions in these factories.

Feelings: Recognizing similarities in humans at the level of desire

Reading

This passage is taken from the novel Oliver Twist. Oliver is a nine-year-old orphan who lives in a badly run orphanage. Unable to bear the ill-treatment and cruelty there, he decides to

run away. Read on to find out what happens next.

'You musn't say you saw me, Dick,' said Oliver. 'I am running away. They beat me and ill-treated me and I'm going to **seek my fortune** a long way off. How pale you look!'

'I'm very glad to see you, Oliver,' said Dick. 'But don't stop, don't stop.'

'Yes, I will say goodbye to you,' said Oliver. 'I know I shall see you again Dick; you will be well and happy.'

'I hope so,' said Dick. He climbed up the low gate and put his little arms around Oliver's neck. 'Goodbye! God bless you!'

This was the first time that anyone had blessed Oliver and through all the trouble and sufferings of his later life he never once forgot it. Oliver walked on to the high road. It was eight o'clock now. He sat down on a **milestone** and began to think for the first time, where he had better go and try to live. The milestone on which he sat showed it was just seventy miles to London. London—that great big city! No one could hopefully find him there! He decided to walk to London.

Oliver walked twenty miles that day. He ate nothing but a crust of dry bread which he had brought along with him. When night came he slept under a haystack in a meadow. Next morning, he felt so hungry that he spent the only penny he had to buy a small loaf of bread.

orphan: a child who has lost both parents

seek (my) fortune: find a way to become rich

milestone: a stone on the road to indicate the distance to a particular place in miles

sore: painful

turnpike: gate set across a road where people have to pay money to pass, like a toll gate

queerest: strangest

bowlegs: legs that curve outwards like a bow

threatened: (here) was in danger of

On what did Oliver spend his penny?

He walked twelve miles that day. His feet were **sore** and his legs so weak that they trembled as he walked. Once more, he slept in the cold, damp air and that made him feel worse. He grew weaker and weaker and were it not for the kindness of a **turnpike** man who gave him bread and cheese, and a generous old lady, who also gave him some food, he would certainly have died along the way.

Early on the seventh morning, he limped into the small town of Barnet. The window panes were closed and the streets were empty. Oliver sat on a doorstep. His feet were bleeding and he was covered with dust. Suddenly he found a boy staring at him. He was one of the **queerest** looking boys Oliver had ever seen. He was short, with **bowlegs** and little, sharp, ugly eyes. But although he was only a boy, he behaved as though he were a man. He wore a large hat on his head which **threatened** to fall off at any moment. He wore a man's coat which reached almost to his heels.

'Hullo, my dear fellow! What's your problem?' said this strange young gentleman to Oliver.

'I am very hungry and tired,' replied Oliver. 'I have walked a long way. I have been walking these seven days.'

'Walking for seven days! Are you running away from prison?'

'No,' replied Oliver.

'Were you ever in jail? Well, never mind. I can see you need some food. I don't have too much money myself but I'll buy you some food and drink. Come on, get up, will you?' said the strange fellow.

He took Oliver to a nearby shop where he bought some bread and meat. He next took him to a pub where Oliver had a **hearty** meal.

'Going to London?' said the strange boy when Oliver had finished.

'Yes,' said Oliver.

'Got a place to stay?'

'No,' said Oliver.

'Money?' asked the boy.

'No,' replied Oliver. The strange boy whistled.

'Do you live in London?' asked Oliver.

'Yes, I do, when I'm home,' said the boy. 'I suppose you want some place to sleep tonight, don't you?'

'I do, indeed,' said Oliver.

'I know a **respectable** old gentleman who lives in London. He'll let you stay in his house and not even charge you for it.'

Oliver discovered that this strange young boy's name was Jack Hawkins, though

Where did the strange fellow take Oliver?

hearty: large

respectable: good and honest

all his friends called him the Artful Dodger. Jack refused to enter London before dark. So it was nearly eleven o'clock before they reached the city. As they walked through the narrow streets, Oliver looked around him and found it was one of the dirtiest places he had ever seen. The air was filled with the smell of **filth**. Oliver was just wondering whether he should run away, when Jack caught him by the arm and pushed him inside a dark passage.

'Now, then!' cried a voice from inside the house in reply to a whistle from the Dodger. 'Plummy and slam!' This seemed to be a **watchword**, for a candle **gleamed** at the end of a passage.

'There are two of you? Who's he?' asked a voice.

'He's a friend,' said the Dodger and led Oliver up some dark and broken stairs. He threw open the door of a room and drew Oliver in after him.

The walls and ceiling of the room were black with age and dirt. An old, **shrivelled** man with a horrible face which was hidden by his dirty red hair stood in front of the fire, frying some meat. The man wore a **greasy flannel** gown. He seemed to be dividing his attention between the meat and a large number of silk handkerchiefs which were hanging on a line. Four or five boys, the same age as the Dodger, were sitting around the table. Several rough beds made from **sack** cloth were placed side by side on the floor.

Wordwise

The word 'artful' means 'sly'. A 'dodger' is someone who uses dishonest methods to get out of difficult situations. Jack Hawkins was called by this name because he was an expert pickpocket.

filth: dirt
watchword: a secret word or phrase used to get entry
gleamed: shone brightly
shrivelled: wrinkled
greasy: oily
flannel: a soft, light woollen fabric
sack: rough cloth made of jute, used to make sacks

What was the watchword to enter the house?

About the author

Charles Dickens (1812–1870) was born in London. His stories and novels describe life in Victorian England, especially the conditions of the poor. Some of his well-known novels are *Nicholas Nickleby* and *Great Expectations*.

Comprehension

Quick Recap

A. Answer the questions in a few lines.

1. Why was Oliver running away?
2. How far did he travel on the first day?
3. Where did he sleep at night?
4. Who showed kindness to Oliver and how?
5. Describe Jack Hawkins' appearance in your own words.
6. Why did Oliver wonder whether he should run away from London?
7. How did Jack Hawkins help Oliver?
8. Describe the old man. What was he doing?

B. Read the lines from the extract and answer the questions.

1. *'I can see you need some food.'*
   a. Who said these words and to whom?
   b. Why did the person spoken to need food?
   c. How far had the person spoken to travelled? For how many days had he been travelling?
2. *'He's a friend,'*
   a. Who said these words and to whom?
   b. Whom does the speaker refer to as 'he'?
   c. What did the speaker do next?

Life Skills and Values — alertness, thinking on one's feet

Think and answer.

1. Describe Jack Hawkins in your own words.
2. Why was a watchword needed to enter the old man's house?

Way with Words

SYNONYMS

A. Underline the correct meaning for each word.

1. **damp:** dry, rough, wet
2. **pale:** weak, thin, poor
3. **suffering:** pain, sadness, hunger
4. **crust:** soft piece, loaf, hard piece
5. **generous:** selfish, kind, happy to share
6. **suppose:** guess, want, give

B. Complete the ladder of verbs, all starting with the letter 'R'. One is done for you.

1. r ___u___ ___n___

2. r _____ _____ _____

3. r _____ _____ _____ _____

4. r _____ _____ _____ _____ _____

5. r _____ _____ _____ _____ _____ _____

Grammar in Use

PREPOSITIONS

Look at the sentence.

Early **on** the seventh morning, Oliver limped **into** the small town **of** Barnet.

The words in bold in the above sentence are prepositions.

Prepositions show the relation between a noun or a pronoun and some other word in a sentence. They give information about position and time.

Some common prepositions are *on*, *at*, *under*, *near*, *over*, *from*, *between*, *before*, *with*, *to*, *beside* and *across*.

A. Complete the sentences with the correct prepositions.

1. The books are ________ the desk. (in/on)
2. Mary walked ________ her mother in the rain. (besides/beside)
3. Sana divided the sweets ________ her friends. (among/between)

4. The table is ________ the bed and the door. (between/among)
5. ________ two cars, Mr Roy also has a motorcycle. (Besides/Beside)
6. Ravi drove the car straight ________ the pillar. (in/into)

Transitive and Intransitive Verbs

Along with a subject, a sentence may also have an object.

The **object** in a sentence is a noun or a pronoun which receives the action of the verb.

We can find the object by asking verb + *whom?* or verb + *what?*

Example: Oliver bought a loaf of **bread**.
Here, the object is **bread**. It answers the question, 'What did Oliver buy?'

A verb which has an object is called a **transitive verb**.

Example: The man **wore** a greasy flannel gown.
Here, 'wore' is the verb and its direct object is 'gown'. So, 'wore' is a transitive verb.

A verb which does not have an object is known as an **intransitive verb**.

Example: I am running away.
Here, the verb 'am running' does not have a direct object. Thus, the verb 'am running' is intransitive. The word 'away' is an adverb, which describes the verb.

B. Underline the verbs in these sentences and say whether they are transitive or intransitive.

1. The Artful Dodger entered London after dark.
2. Every evening, we go for a walk.
3. The child was scared of the neighbour's dog.
4. Reena became a marine scientist.
5. Seema looks unhappy.
6. Mridul opened the door of the room.

Study Skills

Spell Check

Unscramble the following words to form the names of sports.

1. llabtoof ________	4. tekcirc ________	7. carrmo ________
2. hoyeck ________	5. gnitaks ________	8. flog ________
3. sinnet ________	6. yrehcra ________	9. baksetlabl ________

Listening and Speaking

Listen to a short discussion on the topic, 'Oliver made a mistake by running away to London'. Take turns to say which speaker you agree with. You can use the following phrases:

Agree	Disagree
I agree that… It is true that…	I don't agree with you… I don't think that…

Pen it Down

Creativity

What do you think happened after Oliver met the old man and saw where Jack Hawkins lived? Do you think Oliver stayed on to find out what the man and his companions were up to? Did he get scared of the situation and run away again?

Imagine yourself to be in Oliver's place and write a paragraph on what he might have done.

Self Assessment

Now I can

- read and understand a passage about the suffering of those who are not as fortunate as us.
- use synonyms, prepositions, and transitive and intransitive verbs.
- unjumble words, agree or disagree with others politely, and write a paragraph about what happens next in the story.

Read More

David Copperfield: This novel by Charles Dickens follows the life of David, a young boy, who runs away from his cruel stepfather and the terrible conditions of the factory he works in.

Kim: This novel by Rudyard Kipling is about Kim, a British orphan, who lives in the streets in India. Later, he works as a spy for the British Secret Service.

Southeast Asia

folktale

11

The Naga Dragon's Lair

Madhu Gurung

Let's Get Started

In China, Japan and Thailand, the dragon is believed to be a wise and holy spirit who brings luck and prosperity. During the Chinese New Year, people perform the dragon dance, using poles to move a big dragon figure made of bamboo and cloth.

Learn how to make an easy dragon puppet by following these simple instructions.

1. Using the image as reference, draw the head, feet, arms and tail of the dragon on an A4 sheet.
2. Cut out the pieces and colour them.
3. Cut out colourful strips from chart paper to make paper chains.
4. Stick the dragon's face on a strip of coloured paper.
5. Make the paper chain from this piece onwards, linking one strip of paper behind it to the next, like a chain.

6. Stick the arms, legs and tail in place using the image given as reference.
7. You can make the dragon extra-long for fun.
8. Write how you felt after creating this dragon chain. What did you do with it?

HC **Active Participation:** Joy of participation in the collective

Reading

Have you ever helped someone in trouble? Did you expect a reward or praise for helping the person? Read this Burmese folktale about a young man who decides to save the queen of the land, who has been kidnapped by a dragon.

Once upon a time, in the hills of Palaung in Myanmar, there was an old, blind woman. She had a son called Maung Thu Ka Ta. They were very poor and made a living by growing tea. The son was a kind-hearted young man who believed in helping everyone.

One day, the queen of Palaung was carried away by a huge Naga dragon. The whole kingdom was **plunged** in **grief.** The king **issued** a **decree** that any man who rescued his queen and brought her back would be made the crown prince of the land.

How did the old woman and her son make a living?

plunged: thrown
grief: sorrow
issued: gave out
decree: official order

Maung Thu Ka Ta heard the decree and told his mother that he was going to save the queen. His mother nodded her head and went up to their tiny attic and brought him a sword. On the handle of the sword was the carved head of a Naga dragon. Giving it to Maung Thu Ka Ta, his mother said, 'Take this sword. It has been with our family for generations. Its magical powers can kill all snakes and Naga dragons. It will keep you safe.'

Did You Know? Geography

Myanmar (earlier called Burma) is a country located on the border of India and Bangladesh.

Maung Thu Ka Ta went to the king's palace and asked for a basket big enough for someone to sit in comfortably, and a very long and strong rope. Then, along with some of the ministers and soldiers, he came to the opening in the ground through which the dragon had taken the queen.

The hole was very deep. Maung Thu Ka Ta sat in the basket and asked the soldiers to lower him with the help of the rope.

What made the sword unique?

Literary term

1. This is a **simile**. It compares the darkness in the hole with the darkness at night using the word 'as'.

He told the ministers that when he found the queen, he would put her in the basket and tug the rope so that they could pull her up.

As he went down, it became darker. By the time he reached the bottom, it was as dark as night[1]. Exploring the place, Maung Thu Ka Ta found the queen.

'I am a poor man,' he told her. 'I have come to take you back to the palace. Please follow me and I will lead you out of the dragon's **lair**.'

As there was no light in the tunnel, the queen had to hold on to Maung Tha Ka Ta's Shan trousers to follow him. While they were **stumbling** along, a piece of cloth from Maung Thu Ka Ta's trousers, that the queen was holding on to, **frayed** and tore off. Unknowingly, the queen held on to the small piece of torn cloth tightly in her hand.

lair: den

stumbling: walking in an unbalanced way

frayed: wore out

viciously: violently

At last, the two of them reached the basket. The queen sat in it and Maung Thu Ka Ta tugged at the rope. The waiting men recognised the signal and pulled the basket up. They were so overjoyed to see the queen that they forgot to throw back the basket for Maung Thu Ka Ta. They took the queen back to the palace and told the king that they had saved her. The entire kingdom celebrated the return of their queen. But they forgot the man who had gone down the hole and rescued her.

While escaping, what was the queen holding on to?

Did You Know? G.K.

Shan trousers are loose pants, with a thick waistband. They were once worn only by fishermen in Thailand but are quite popular today.

Meanwhile, Maung Thu Ka Ta realised that he was trapped. He sat down to wait for the dragon with his sword. When the dragon returned and found that the queen had disappeared, he hissed in anger. He saw Maung Thu Ka Ta and attacked him **viciously**. But Maung Thu Ka Ta was ready with his sword.

After a fierce fight, he managed to kill the dragon. Then he found another hole going further down.

Sliding down the hole, Maung Thu Ka Ta found himself in a new land. It was lit up brightly and had trees full of gold and silver fruits. The houses had walls **studded** with bright red rubies.

Maung Thu Ka Ta was at once surrounded by **ferocious** Naga dragons and taken prisoner. He was brought before the king who asked Maung Thu Ka Ta the reason for his visit to their country. As he was an honest man, he told the king everything. The king looked at him carefully and realised that he was telling the truth. Instead of killing him, he held a feast and ordered all the Naga dragons to come in their human form.

studded: decorated with raised objects

ferocious: fierce

instructed: ordered

rewarded: given a prize

At the feast, the king said, 'Maung Thu Ka Ta, I have decided not to kill you because you are a good man. You look after your old mother and you took up the challenge to save your queen. I will give you a big ruby that is equal to a king's treasure and send you back to your land.' Maung Thu Ka Ta thanked the king and bade him farewell.

What did the Naga King gift Maung Thu Ka Ta?

Meanwhile at the palace, the queen was very sad. The king asked her what it was that made her so upset.

She replied, 'These ministers did not save me from the dragon. Although I never saw the face of the man who saved me, I know it was not one of them.'

The queen told the king about the torn piece of cloth she had, which belonged to her rescuer. The king thought for a while and said, 'I will hold a big festival at the palace for seven days and invite all the young men of the kingdom. Then, you can find the man by matching the cloth with his trousers.'

At the festival, the king **instructed** his guards to bring all the young men to the palace, especially anyone wearing torn Shan pants. Six days passed, but the queen did not find anyone wearing trousers matching the torn piece of cloth.

For how long did the festival continue?

On the seventh and last day of the festival, Maung Thu Ka Ta returned from the land of the Naga dragons and came to the palace. The guards saw that his pants were torn. They immediately took him to the queen, who sat in court with the king. The queen brought the piece of cloth. It matched Maung Thu Ka Ta's trousers perfectly.

The queen was overjoyed. She addressed the entire court and said, 'I always wanted the right man to be **rewarded**. The ministers don't know that while I was following the man who heir: someone who will receive a person's money or property when that person dies

rescued me, a piece from his trousers tore and stayed in my hand. I knew that he was not a rich man, but one with a brave heart. Today, we have found him.'

The king, too, was very happy. He crowned Maung Thu Ka Ta his **heir**. The young man sent for his mother and they all lived happily in the palace.

How was Maung Thu Ka Ta rewarded by the king?

About the author

Madhu Gurung is a writer based in Dehradun. 'The Naga Dragon's Lair' is from the book, *Burmese Folktales*, that she wrote when she lived in Myanmar.

Comprehension

Quick Recap

A. Answer the questions in a few lines.

1. Why were the people of Palaung plunged in grief?
2. What decree was issued by the king?
3. What did Maung Thu Ka Ta's mother give him and why?
4. Why did Maung Thu Ka Ta ask for a basket and a rope?
5. What happened when the Naga dragon returned to his lair?
6. Why did the king of the dragons decide not to kill Maung Thu Ka Ta?
7. Why was the queen sad after being rescued?
8. How did the king of Palaung plan to find the man who saved the queen?

B. Read the lines from the story and answer the questions.

1. *'I am a poor man.'*

a. Who said these words and to whom?

b. Where was the speaker at that moment?

c. Why had the speaker gone there?

2. *'Today we have found him.'*

a. Who said these words and to whom?

b. Who does the word 'him' refer to?

c. Why was the speaker happy to have found him?

Life Skills and Values bravery, honesty

Think and answer.

1. Why did Maung Thu Ka Ta decide to save the queen?
2. How do we know that the ministers and the soldiers were dishonest?
3. What qualities did Maung Thu Ka Ta have that helped him become rich and successful?

Way with Words

Similes

A. You have come across an example of a simile in this chapter. Complete the following similes using the words from the box.

bird	lead	fox	honey	feather
kitten	coal	lion	bat	lamb

1. as black as ____________
2. as brave as a ____________
3. as blind as a ____________
4. as heavy as ____________
5. as sweet as ____________
6. as cunning as a ____________
7. as free as a ____________
8. as gentle as a ____________
9. as light as a ____________
10. as playful as a ____________

B. Create your own similes by completing the following expressions.

1. as old as ____________
2. as white as ____________
3. as slow as ____________
4. as sharp as ____________
5. as green as ____________
6. as sweet as ____________

Objects and Their Sounds

C. Match the objects with the sounds they make.

A	B
1. keys	a. rustle
2. clocks	b. clatter
3. doors	c. ring
4. bells	d. bang
5. wind	e. tick tock
6. leaves	f. howls

Grammar in Use

Types of Adjectives

Look at these sentences.

One day, the queen of Palaung was carried away by a **huge** Naga dragon.

The word **huge** is an example of an **adjective of quality** as it describes the size of the dragon.

I will hold a big festival at the palace for **seven** days.

The word **seven** is an example of an **adjective of number** as it tells us the duration of the festival, which is seven days.

His mother offered us **some** tea that she had grown.

The word **some** is an example of an **adjective of quantity** as it tells us the amount of tea offered.

A. Underline the adjective in each sentence and state its type.

1. The friendly boy settled in his new school quickly.
2. There was enough rice in the pot to feed the whole family.
3. We went on a trip to Rajasthan for twelve days.
4. The builders poured some sand into the pit.
5. I received nine gifts on my birthday.
6. Avoid looking directly at the bright sun.

Types of Adverbs

Look at these sentences.

The queen held on to the cloth **tightly**.

The Naga dragon's lair was **inside** the kingdom of Palaung.

Maung Thu Ka Ta set off to find the queen **today**.

The words in bold in these sentences are adverbs.

An **adverb** is a word which tells us more about a verb.

The word **tightly** describes *how* the queen held on to the cloth.
It is an **adverb of manner**. Such adverbs describe how something happens.

The word **inside** describes *where* the Naga dragon's lair was.
It is an **adverb of place**. Such adverbs describe where something happens.

The word **today** tells us *when* Maung Thu Ka Ta set off to find the queen.
It is an **adverb of time**. Such adverbs describe when something happens.

B. Underline the adverbs in these sentences and state what type they are.

1. The sun shines brightly.
2. The athlete lost the race today.
3. The principal proudly said that the school had come first in the inter-school quiz competition.
4. The ice cream seller is nearby. I can hear his bell.
5. The soldiers fought bravely in the battle.
6. We must cross the road carefully.
7. I searched everywhere for my friend, but could not find him.
8. The organisers will start the programme now.

Study Skills

Use Your Dictionary

Find the following words in your dictionary and write their meanings. Then, use the words to make sentences of your own.

1. rescuer   2. attic   3. farewell   4. feast   5. triumph   6. guardian   7. treasurer

Listening and Speaking

A. Listen to a passage about a naughty boy and complete the paragraph.

Aunt Polly had a naughty nephew called ____________. They lived in the town of ____________. On ____________, he ran away from school and dirtied his clothes in a ____________. As a punishment, his aunt made him ____________ the next day. Being a clever boy, he made his friends agree to exchange their ____________ with him for the honour of doing his work. He then exchanged these for tickets given out in ____________ and later, he used the tickets to win a ____________ as a prize.

B. You read about the way Maung Thu Ka Ta rescued the queen and killed the dragon. In groups of four, discuss and speak in class about another way in which he could have rescued the queen.

21ST CENTURY Communication

Pen it Down

21ST CENTURY Creativity

Imagine that you are on a school trip to a hill station. You fall behind along the way and get lost. While trying to find your way back, you come across a large, crumbling house. You are curious to know who lives inside and enter the house.

Write a short account of your experience. Give your story a title.

Self Assessment

Now I can

- read and understand a folktale about facing a difficult situation with courage.
- use similes, and recognize types of adjectives and adverbs.
- participate in a class discussion and write an account about my experiences.

Read More

How to Train Your Dragon: This is the first book in a series by Cressida Cowell, about a boy who tries to catch and train a dragon. It has been made into an animated film for children.

Arabian Nights: This is a collection of folktales from the Arabian Peninsula that include 'Sinbad, the Sailor', 'Aladdin and the Magic Lamp', and 'Ali Baba and the Forty Thieves'.

12

The Sound Collector

Roger McGough

Let's Get Started

Does your daily routine differ during the weekdays and on the weekend? Look carefully at these daily routine clocks and see how you spend your day during the week and on the weekend. In your notebook, write the activities that you do on weekdays and on weekends during the times shown in these two clocks. A few have been done for you.

Learning and Awareness: Material vs people

Reading

What are the various sounds that you hear on your way to school? What would it be like if you had to wear earplugs that would block out all sounds for a day? Read a poem

When did the stranger call?

Literary term

1. The words 'purring' and 'ticking' are examples of **onomatopoeia**. A kitten's call sounds just like the word 'purr'. The movement of a clock's hands sounds just like the word 'tick' being repeated.

in which all the sounds of a busy house are taken away by a mysterious stranger.

A stranger called this morning
Dressed all in black and grey
Put every sound into a bag
And carried them away

The whistling of the kettle
The turning of the lock
The purring[1] of the kitten
The ticking of the clock

The popping of the toaster
The crunching of the **flakes**
When you spread the marmalade
The scraping noise it makes

The hissing of the frying pan
The ticking of the **grill**
The bubbling of the bathtub
As it starts to fill

The drumming of the raindrops
On the windowpane
When you do the washing-up
The gurgle of the drain

The crying of the baby
The squeaking of the chair
The swishing of the curtain
The creaking of the stair

A stranger called this morning
He didn't leave his name
Left us only silence
Life will never be the same.

Did You Know? G. K.

Marmalade is a jam made with the peels of the orange, instead of the fruit pulp. Originally, it was made from quince, a pear-like fruit.

flakes: (here) cornflakes

grill: a device inside an oven

About the poet

Roger McGough (1937–) is a British poet and playwright. He often performs his poetry in front of an audience.

Comprehension

Quick Recap

A. Answer the questions in a few lines.

1. What was the stranger wearing?
2. What was he carrying? What did he put in it?
3. Make a list of all the objects in the house and the sounds they make.
4. When does the bathtub make a sound?
5. Why will life never be the same again in the house?
6. Give two examples of onomatopoeia from the poem.

B. Read the lines from the poem and answer the questions.

1. *When you spread the marmalade ...*
   a. What is marmalade?
   b. Where do we spread it?
   c. What is the sound made when you spread marmalade?

2. *The gurgle of the drain*
   a. What sound is being referred to in the given line?
   b. What makes this sound?
   c. Write down two more words which refer to the sound of flowing water.

3. *He didn't leave his name*
   a. Who is being referred to as 'he'?
   b. What did he leave behind instead of his name?
   c. What did 'he' do at the house?

Life Skills and Values — being observant

Think and answer.

1. Write four sentences about the house which the poem describes.
2. Who do you think the sound collector is? Why did he not leave his name?

Way with Words

Sound Words

A. Find and circle ten sound words in the word grid.

S	P	L	A	T	T	E	R	A	B	K	M
C	J	I	H	G	F	E	U	D	C	U	X
R	K	L	M	N	O	P	S	Q	R	W	F
E	T	S	S	R	A	T	T	L	E	T	I
E	U	M	V	W	X	Y	L	Z	A	Y	R
C	G	A	F	E	D	C	E	B	G	F	G
H	I	S	H	J	K	L	M	N	I	U	J
R	W	H	O	O	P	Q	P	O	G	X	I
H	S	T	U	V	W	X	Y	Z	G	T	T
I	D	C	B	A	G	R	O	W	L	B	V
S	G	U	R	G	L	E	K	L	E	Z	I
S	M	A	C	K	Q	P	O	N	M	O	Y

Imagery

Imagery makes use of words in a way that appeals to our five senses.

Examples: Dressed all in black and grey.
Here, the words 'black and grey' appeal to the sense of sight.
The crying of the baby.
Here, the word 'crying' appeals to the sense of hearing.

B. Underline the words in these sentences which create an image. Then, mention which sense it appeals to.

1. The children were shouting in the classroom.
2. The juicy mangoes are very sweet.
3. The fragrance of the rose filled the room.
4. The boy got lost in the dark and dense forest.
5. Maya wore a dress made of soft silk.

Grammar in Use

PAST CONTINUOUS TENSE

A verb is said to be in the **past continuous tense** when it describes an ongoing action in the past.

Examples: The baby **was crying** because it was hungry.
A stranger **was ringing** the bell in the morning.

A. Complete the sentences with the past continuous form of the given verbs.

1. My grandmother ____________ a cardigan for me. (knit)
2. A gentle breeze ____________ when I woke up. (blow)
3. The teacher ____________ the stairs with a pile of books in her hand. (climb)
4. Ravi ____________ his clothes when the bell rang. (put on)
5. Raveena ____________ dinner all by herself yesterday. (eat)
6. The young boy ____________ behind the tree. (hide)

TENSES

B. Complete the sentences with the correct form of the given verbs.

1. The parcel ____________ tomorrow evening. (arrive)
2. What ____________ you ____________ when I called? (do)
3. I had completed my work before I ____________ out to play. (go)
4. He ____________ a glass of milk every morning. (drink)
5. My father ____________ the mobile phone bill yesterday. (pay)
6. I ____________ a new pen next week. (buy)

Study Skills

Pronounce Well

WORDS OFTEN MISPRONOUNCED

Look at the words in bold in these sentences. They have the same consonants at the beginning and in the end. However, they are pronounced differently and have different meanings. We often confuse their pronunciation.

1. **Sit** in your **seat**.

2. We used some **flour** to bake a loaf of bread. But the bread fell on the **floor**.
3. **Leave** him so that he can **live**.
4. The **ship** is carrying a flock of **sheep**.
5. Don't eat your **dessert** in the **desert**.

Listen to your teacher as she/he reads out these sentences. Pay attention to the words in bold. Next, practise saying these words with the correct pronunciation.

Listening and Speaking

A. Listen to various sounds from our daily life. Identify them and write them down.

B. Listen to the sounds again. Work in pairs and say whether you would consider them as noise or as a pleasant sound. Give reasons for your answer.

Pen it Down

What are the various sounds you hear at home, from the time you get up to the moment when you leave for school? Do they make you happy, sad or angry? Why?

Write a paragraph on the topic.

HC Recognizing characteristics and nature of entities

Self Assessment

Now I can

- read a poem about the various sounds which form a part of our daily lives.
- identify sound words and imagery.
- practise the different tenses, including past continuous tense.
- correctly pronounce often-mispronounced words, identify and classify sounds, and write a paragraph.

Read More

Farmyard Song: This poem by J. T. Trowbridge talks about the various sights and sounds of life on a farm.

Fabulous Beast: This poem by Sampurna Chattarji is about a truck that comes to collect garbage from the poet's neighbourhood. It is imagined as a living beast that eats garbage and spits it out in the dump.

Be Creative!

SUSTAINABLE DEVELOPMENT GOALS 15 LIFE ON LAND

A. In the story 'A Crow in the House', the narrator and his grandfather saved a crow which had been injured. What would you do to help a hurt bird or animal? Write a short story using the hints given below.

walking back from school – heard cries of an animal – found the injured animal – used handkerchief to bandage the wound – brought home – nursed to health – adopted as pet

B. Read the sentences and choose the part that has the preposition.

1. Ram stood near the window and watched the sun rise over the distant mountains.
   - ☐ Ram stood near the window
   - ☐ over the distant mountains
   - ☐ the sun rise
   - ☐ and watched
2. Jaya cleaned her room and put everything inside the cupboard.
   - ☐ and put everything
   - ☐ Jaya cleaned
   - ☐ her room and
   - ☐ inside the cupboard
3. Ravi leaned his bicycle against the fence.
   - ☐ against the fence
   - ☐ his bicycle
   - ☐ Ravi leaned
4. We often go for a walk along the river bank.
   - ☐ We often
   - ☐ go for a walk
   - ☐ along the river bank

C. Draw one mechanical object that you have at home, like the clock in the poem 'The Sound Collector'. Write five interesting facts about the object.

ART INTEGRATION

____

____

____

____

____

13 The Wizard of Oz

Lyman Frank Baum

Let's Get Started

Experiences can be of many types. Some experiences are full of adventure and bring us joy. Some, like misfortunes, cause us pain. There are also experiences that teach us something new.

Read and sort the following experiences into the three types given in the table.

losing a pet and finding it again
misplacing an expensive watch
missing a train or flight
receiving poor grades in tests
solving a mystery
going on a treasure hunt
fighting with one's best friend
learning a recipe from Grandma
going rock climbing

Adventure	Misfortune	Learning

HC **Feelings:** Responsibility towards others

Reading

Dorothy lived with her uncle and aunt in the state of Kansas, USA. One day, a furious cyclone blew Dorothy, her dog Toto and their house into the magical land of Oz. The house landed on the Evil Witch of the West, killing her. But when Dorothy wanted to return home, she learned that her only way was to go to Emerald City and ask for the help of the great and powerful Wizard of Oz. Read on to find out what happens on the way there.

On the way to Emerald City, three friends joined Dorothy.
If I go with you, will Oz give me some brains? If my head stays **stuffed** with straw, how will I ever know anything?
The Scarecrow
Do you suppose Oz could give me a heart? I was tricked into this tin body by an evil witch. I want a heart to feel love again.
The Tin Woodman
The last to join them was the Cowardly Lion, the king of the jungle.
The Cowardly Lion
Do you think Oz could give me **courage**? I may be king, but I am terrified of everyone, even elephants, tigers and bears. I'm such a coward.
The road to Emerald City was through a thick forest. The friends didn't know it then, but the journey would test them all. At night, the travellers camped under a large tree. The Tin Woodman chopped a heap of wood, with which Dorothy built a **crackling** fire.
If you are hungry, my friend, I will kill a deer for you.
Oh, please don't! I will cry if you kill a poor deer. Then my jaws would rust and I wouldn't be able to move them.
For a man without a heart, the Woodman was very **sensitive**.
While the Lion went away to find its own meal, the Scarecrow found a tree full of nuts for Dorothy. He also covered her with a pile of dry leaves to keep her **snug** and warm.
Thank you, dear Scarecrow. How kind and thoughtful you are!
Now you don't have to worry about your next meal.

The next morning, they reached a great **ditch**. It divided the forest as far as they could see on either side. It was wide and very deep, with many big, **jagged** rocks at the bottom.
What shall we do?
I don't have the slightest idea!
We can't climb down into the ditch. The sides are too **steep**. We cannot jump over it either. We must stop here.
I think I could jump over it.
It was decided that the Lion could carry them on his back, one at a time.

I will go first. If you couldn't make it across, Dorothy would be killed or the Tin Woodman badly bent on the sharp rocks below. But if I fall, I wouldn't get hurt at all.
I am terribly afraid of falling, myself. But there is nothing to do but to try.
For a cowardly Lion, he was being very courageous indeed.

With the Scarecrow on his back, the Lion **crouched** down and gave a great **spring**.
He shot through the air and landed safely on the other side, to the cheers of his friends.

Next, the Lion sprang across the ditch with Dorothy and Toto, and finally the Woodman. They all reached the other side safely.
The forest was very dark and **gloomy**.
They heard strange noises deep inside the woods.
What is that noise?
GRRRRRR
They are the Kalidahs, **monstrous** beasts with claws so long and sharp that they could tear me in two without a second thought. I'm terribly afraid of the Kalidahs.
Suddenly, they came upon a **gulf** across the road. But it was so broad and deep that the Lion knew at once he could not leap across it. Again, the Scarecrow found a solution.
Look at this great tree. If the Woodman can chop it down, so that it falls to the other side, we can use it as a bridge to walk across.
That is a first-rate idea! One might think you had brains in your head, instead of straw.
The Woodman set to work at once, and so sharp was his axe that the tree was soon chopped down.
CRASH!
The Lion pushed the tree with all his might. It tipped and fell across the ditch.
They were crossing this strange bridge when a sharp growl made them look back.
The Kalidahs!
Quick! Let us cross over.

The Lion was terrified, but he knew he had to save his friends.
Ruh?
GRRRRRR
The Lion's roar was so loud and terrible that Dorothy screamed and the Scarecrow fell over. Even the **fierce** beasts stopped and looked at him in surprise.
But the Kalidahs were bigger than the Lion. They were two while the Lion was one. They rushed forward.
We are lost. They will tear us to pieces with their sharp claws. But stand close behind me, and I will fight them as long as I am alive.
Wait a minute! I have a plan. Woodman, can you chop away that tree, on our side?
Oh, yes!
The Tin Woodman began chopping away at once. The Kalidahs were nearly across, when the tree crashed into the gulf, carrying the **snarling** beasts with it.
Well, I see we are going to live a little while longer. Those creatures frightened me so badly that my heart is beating like a drum.
I wish I had a heart to beat.
The travellers were now **anxious** to get out of the forest. They walked as fast as they could.
By afternoon, they had left the forest behind. Beyond the river lay the beautiful country of Oz where they would continue their journey.

stuffed: filled

courage: quality of being ready to do something dangerous, even though you are afraid

crackling: sharp sounds from a bright fire

sensitive: being able to understand other people's feelings

snug: comfortable and cosy

ditch: a narrow waterbody with flowing water

jagged: rough with sharp edges

steep: rising or falling sharply

crouched: sat down on all fours

spring: sudden jump

gloomy: dark and sad

monstrous: something scary like a monster

gulf: a deep and wide gap

fierce: (here) dangerous and ready to attack

snarling: growling angrily with teeth showing

anxious: worried

About the author

Lyman Frank Baum (1856–1919) was an American author best-known for *The Wonderful Wizard of Oz* and the 13 books that continued the story. Baum took up many jobs, like raising chickens, writing plays and running a theatre company, before becoming a writer.

Comprehension

Quick Recap

A. Answer these questions.

1. Where was Dorothy going?
2. Who joined her on the way?
3. What did the Scarecrow want from Oz and why?
4. Mention the two things the Scarecrow did for Dorothy.
5. How did they cross the ditch?
6. What happened when the lion roared loudly?

B. Read the lines from the story and answer the questions.

1. *Do you suppose Oz could give me a heart?*
   a. Who said these words and to whom?
   b. Why did the speaker need a heart? How did he lose his heart?
   c. What did the next speaker want from Oz?

2. *They live in these parts.*
   a. Who does 'they' refer to?

b. Describe the ones being referred to as 'they'.

c. Who is afraid of them and why?

Life Skills and Values accepting oneself, being courageous

Think and answer.

1. Do you think the Lion was a brave animal? Give examples from the story.
2. Did the Scarecrow, the Woodman and the Lion already have the qualities they wanted from the Wizard of Oz? Give reasons for your answer.
3. Of the three characters – the Scarecrow, the Woodman and the Lion – whom do you like the most and why?

Way with Words

A. Tick the correct meanings of the words in bold.

1. The word **tricked** means
   a. deceived. b. played. c. decided.
2. Another way of saying 'he is a **coward**' is
   a. 'he is afraid of most things'. b. 'he is bold and strong'. c. 'he is slow but steady'.
3. The word **strange** can be replaced with the word
   a. known. b. unusual. c. expected.
4. The antonym of **sharp** is
   a. pointed. b. blunt. c. quick.
5. The meaning of the word **camped** is
   a. travelled somewhere. b. built a house. c. stayed somewhere for a short time

Anagrams

You have learnt that an anagram is a word formed by rearranging the letters of another word.

Example: snug → guns

B. Write the anagrams of these words using the clues given.

1. horse ______________ (place where sea meets land)
2. bread ______________ (hair on the face)
3. paws ______________ (an insect that stings)

4. large __________ (an angry stare)
5. east __________ (a place to sit)
6. listen __________ (another word for 'quiet')
7. late __________ (another word for 'story')
8. rested __________ (a place with little or no rain)

Binomial Pairs

C. Complete the following phrases with the given words.

down	knife	butter	bone	cheese	low	white	roll

1. chalk and __________
2. rock and __________
3. up and __________
4. skin and __________
5. black and __________
6. bread and __________
7. high and __________
8. fork and __________

Grammar in Use

Phrases

A group of words without a subject and a predicate is called a **phrase**. A phrase adds meaning to a sentence and often begins with a preposition.

Example: Dororthy and Toto were gone **for some time**.

The phrase 'for some time' gives us information about Dorothy and Toto.

A. Complete the following sentences using these phrases.

under the tree	down the street
at the clown's tricks	on the wall
along the beach	behind the curtain

1. We all laughed __________.
2. The boy hid __________.
3. They are walking __________.
4. The children sat __________.
5. The clock __________ has stopped working.
6. The band of musicians marched __________.

Apostrophe to show possession

You know that an **apostrophe** (') is used to show that someone or something belongs or relates to someone or something else.

We add an apostrophe s (**'s**) at the end of singular words or personal names.
Examples: the Woodman**'s** axe, Dorothy**'s** dress, the dog**'s** collar

We add an apostrophe s (**'s**) at the end of plurals that do not end in **s**.
Examples: children**'s** games, women**'s** clothes, people**'s** houses

We use only apostrophe (') with names that already end in **s**.
Examples: James' car, Charles' garden

We use only apostrophe (') with plurals that already end in **s**.
Examples: the students' books, the teachers' room

B. Rewrite the sentences by replacing the expressions in italics. One is done for you.

1. This *book belongs to Sara*.
   This is **Sara's** book.
2. This is a *meeting for teachers*.
3. This is *the cat that belongs to Alisha*.
4. We read a story about *the magic lamp of Aladdin*.
5. *The surface of the sun* is very hot.
6. We always enjoy *stories told by Grandma*.
7. The *bat belonging to the child* is lost.
8. Jayant is going to *the house which belongs to his uncle*.

We should not confuse possessive nouns with the plural form of nouns. Remember that for plural nouns, the apostrophe will come after the noun. For example:

The lion's manes were brown in colour. ✗
The lions' manes were brown in colour. ✓

C. Rewrite the following sentences after adding the apostrophe in the correct places.

1. Riya took a book from Prabhas bag.
2. Mrs Sinha teaches at a womens college.
3. We went for a picnic in Siyas car.
4. The hotels staff was very helpful.
5. The shop only sells womens bags.

Study Skills

Spell Check

Circle all the misspelt words in the grid. Then, write the correct spellings.

friends	coward	stuffed	heap	crakling
forest	sensitive	jagged	afriad	crouched
brige	instead	crash	foward	snarling
adventure	chopping	pieces	anxious	screamed
suprise	fierce	beyond	thining	journey
beautiful	cretures	continue	terribley	fritened

Listening and Speaking

A. Listen to a passage from *The Wizard of Oz* and fill in the blanks.

1. The ____________ and the ____________ had changed Aunt Em.
2. They had taken the ____________ from her cheeks and left them gray.
3. Aunt Em was startled by Dorothy's ____________.
4. Uncle Henry did not know what ____________ was.
5. He looked serious and he hardly ever ____________.

B. In groups of four, enact an imaginary conversation between the four friends in which they remember how they escaped from the Kalidahs. You can use the suggestions in the help box.

21st Century Communication

What is that noise?	I am terribly scared of them.	What a wonderful idea!
They are the Kalidahs.	How do we cross the gulf?	Quick! Let us cross over.
We can use a tree to make a bridge to cross the gulf.		

Pen it Down

21st Century Creativity

Imagine that back home, Dorothy has gone missing. Her uncle and aunt want to put up a poster to search for her. Create a poster asking for help to find Dorothy. You can include the following points in the poster:

- where and when she was last seen, and in the company of her pet dog
- her age and how she looks

- the clothes she was wearing at the time, and any birthmarks
- the reward for finding her

Self Assessment

Now I can

- read and understand a story about a girl who finds new friends on her journey back home.
- practise anagrams, binomial pairs, phrases and the apostrophe used to show possession.
- correct misspelt words, enact a conversation on a given topic and make a poster.

Read More

The Adventures of Dunno and his Friends: This book, part of a series by Nikolay Nosov, is about Dunno, a boy who lives with his friends in Flower City. They build a hot air balloon to go on an adventure.

Five on a Treasure Island: This is the first book in a series by Enid Blyton, about four cousins and their dog, Timothy, as they hunt for treasure on a wrecked ship off Kirrin Island.

14

The Lighthouse

Marjorie Wilson

Let's Get Started

Match the following words related to sailing with their descriptions.

'Sailing' words	Meaning
port	person who works as a sailor but is low in rank
buoy	small boat carried on a ship, used to escape if the ship is in danger of sinking
seaman	word used by sailors to call out to each other
sail	town or city with a harbour where ships can load and unload goods
lifeboat	floating object, which marks dangerous places in the sea
lighthouse	strong cloth that helps a boat or ship move with the wind
Ahoy!	tower by the sea that shines a bright light to warn ships of danger

HC **Active Participation:** Distinctions and interrelations of entities

Reading

Have you ever seen a lighthouse? A lighthouse has a powerful flashing lamp for guiding ships. It gives out a flashing beam of light and acts like a traffic signal at sea. Read this

poem about the life of a lighthouse keeper.

Burning upon some hidden shore
Across the sea one night
('A little **reef**,' the Captain said),
We saw a shining light.

He said there was a lighthouse there
Where, lonely in the sea,
Men lived to guard that moving light,
And **trim** the lamp for me.

For me, for him, for every ship
That passes by that way.
I thought it must be strange and quiet
To be there every day.

They have no shops, no fields, no streets;
No whispering sound of trees,
But always shouting at their feet
The great voice of the seas.[1]

And when we sleep at night they wake,
And over every wave
They send that straight strong arm of light
Stretched like a rope to save.

What is the voice heard there at all times?

Literary term

1. This is an example of **personification**. The sound of the waves lashing against the lighthouse is imagined as a person shouting at the top of his voice.

reef: long line of rocks just above or below the surface of water

trim: cut away the burnt parts of the string or cloth in a candle or lamp

About the poet

Marjorie Wilson was an English poet who wrote under the pen name 'Town Girl'. Some of her poems are 'To Tony' and 'The Gates to England'.

Comprehension

Quick Recap

A. Answer the questions in a few lines.

1. What did the speaker see across the sea one night?
2. Who lived and worked there? What work did he do?
3. Why did the speaker think that that person's life was 'strange and quiet'?
4. What do the people of this profession do while others are asleep?

B. Read the lines from the poem and answer the questions.

1. *He said there was a lighthouse there*
   a. Who does the word 'he' refer to?
   b. Who was in the lighthouse?
   c. Where was the speaker?

2. *They send that straight strong arm of light*
   Stretched like a rope to save.
   a. Who sends the arm of light?
   b. Who does it save and how?
   c. Explain the simile used in these lines.

Life Skills and Values — appreciating hard work

Think and answer.

1. What do you think would happen if there was no one to guard the lighthouse?
2. According to you, who is the speaker in the poem? Give reasons.

21st Century Critical Thinking

Way with Words

Nautical Words

A. Make a list of all the words related to the sea and sailing in the poem.

B. Add a letter to make a new word.

a. man____	c. bake____	e. ____pill	g. ____how
b. was____	d. ____race	f. dam____	h. brow____

Grammar in Use

Participles: Present and Past

A **participle** is formed from the base form of a verb. It can be used as an adjective.

The **present participle** always ends in '-ing' while the **past participle** ends in *-ed*, *-d*, *-t*, *-on* or *-n*.

Examples: They have no shops, no fields, no streets;
No **whispering** sound of trees,

The word 'whispering' acts as an adjective and describes the sound made by the trees. It is a present participle.

As the ship went down, the sailor held on to
the **stretched** rope with all his might.

The word 'stretched' describes the rope.
It is a past participle.

The past participle can also form a part of verbs.

Example: The captain had **spoken** to the sailors about his plans.
Here, 'had spoken' is the complete verb. The word 'spoken' is a past participle which forms part of the verb.

Sometimes, the simple past tense and the past participle forms of a verb are the same.

Example: Trisha **lost** her purse today.
Peter found the **lost** book.

A. Underline the participles. State whether they are present or past participles.

1. There are stolen objects in the truck.
2. I don't want to eat that burnt slice of cake.
3. Ravi couldn't finish the boring story.
4. The swinging door made a terrible noise.
5. The galloping horse jumped over the fence easily.
6. Barking dogs are not always dangerous.

B. Complete the sentences with the present participle form of the given verbs.

1. The ____________ cat purred and twitched its tail. (sleep)
2. The ____________ map led the detectives away from the correct path. (confuse)

3. My sister was so impressed by the __________ doll that she longed to have one. (dance)

4. The __________ parrot was the main attraction of the pet shop. (sing)

5. The man tried to jump onto a __________ bus and hurt himself. (run)

C. Complete the sentences with the past participle form of the given verbs.

1. Have you __________ the train ticket? (book)
2. She has finally __________ after two years in Australia. (return)
3. We have not __________ her since yesterday. (see)
4. Rohan has __________ his book again. (lose)
5. Have you ever __________ the President of India? (meet)
6. My school team has never __________ a match. (win)

Study Skills

Pronounce Well

You know that **homophones** are words which have different spelling but similar pronunciation.

Listen carefully and repeat each pair of homophones.

ate – eight	for – four	morning – mourning	blew – blue
aunt – aren't	spot – sport	allowed – aloud	heel – hill

Do you know the meanings of all these words? Use your dictionary to find out the meanings of the words that you don't know.

Listening and Speaking

Listen to a teacher informing students about the rules to be followed in school.

Now, imagine that you are the junior school captain. You have to inform the students about the school rules at the next assembly. Make a speech, informing them of the school rules.

You can start your speech by talking about the following rules:

- Students should wear clean and neatly-ironed uniforms.
- Students should reach school on time. If someone is late, they should bring a letter from their parents, explaining the reason for the delay.

Speak about ten such rules.

Pen it Down

Creativity

Your class is organising a cultural programme to recognise the efforts of people who help us in our day-to-day lives. You want to invite a lighthouse guard for the programme. Design an invitation card inviting him/her to the event.

You should include the following points in your card:

- the name of the programme
- the theme of the programme
- the performances which will be a part of the programme
- the venue, date and time

HC Gratitude and respect

Self Assessment

Now I can

- read and understand a poem about the work done by the lighthouse keeper to keep others safe.
- identify nautical words, and use present and past participles.
- make a speech and design an invitation card.

Read More

Paper Boats: This poem by Rabindranath Tagore is about a young boy who floats paper boats with his name and the name of his village written on them. He hopes these boats will be found by someone in a strange land.

Where Go the Boats?: This poem by Robert Louis Stevenson is about a child thinking of the places where the paper boats will go.

15

How the Leopard Got His Spots

Rudyard Kipling

Let's Get Started

Folktales teach us how to lead our lives in a better way and solve everyday problems. Read this well-known folktale of the blue jackal from the *Panchatantra* and complete the story map in your notebook. Add the moral of the story.

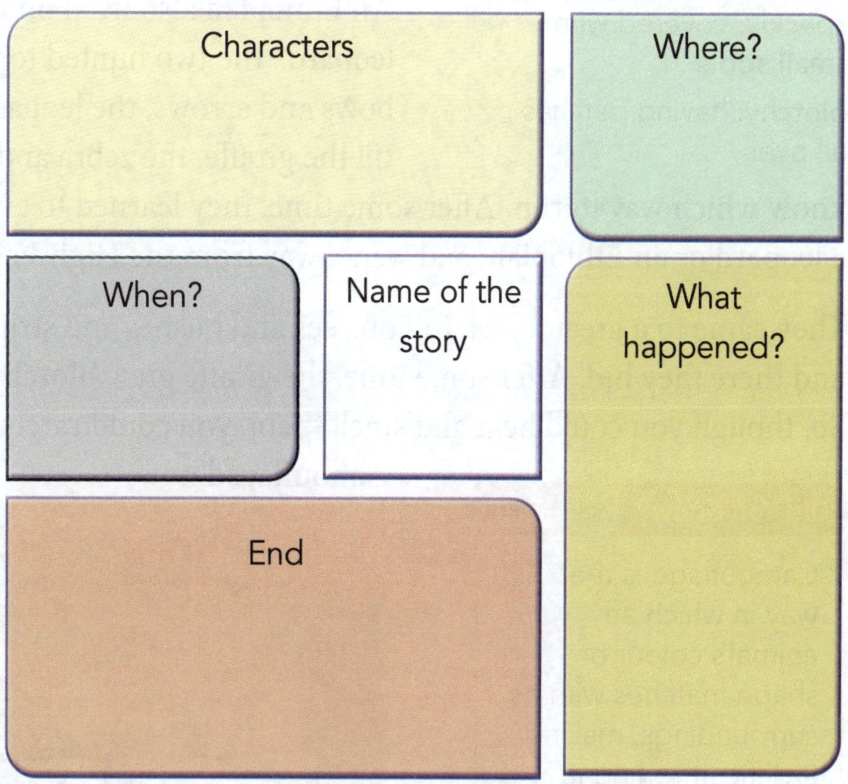

There was once a jackal who lived in a forest near a village. One day, he thought of going to a village nearby to steal some food. As he was about to enter a man's house, the village guard dogs started barking and chasing him. The jackal ran through the village to save himself, but by mistake, he entered the yard of a man who coloured clothes for a living. There was a tub of bright blue colour in the yard. The jackal fell into the tub, and the colour coated him from top to toe. He became a blue jackal! The dogs did not recognise him and ran past him. The jackal was saved, but he decided never to return to the village to steal food.

HC **Active Participation:** Recognising characteristics and intrinsic nature of entities

Reading

Do you wonder why we all look different even though we have the the same facial features? While some animals have stripes on their skin, some have patches and yet others have spots. Read this story which explains how this happened.

Where did the leopard live when the world began?

Veldt: open grasslands in southern Africa

tufts: bunches

Ethiopian: a person from the country of Ethiopia in Africa

speckly: covered with small spots

blotchy: having patches all over

In the days when the world began, the leopard lived in a place called the High **Veldt**, where there was sand, rock and **tufts** of sandy-yellowish grass. The giraffe and the zebra lived there too; and they were sandy-yellow-brownish all over. But the leopard was the sandiest of them all and matched the colour of the High Veldt to one hair. This was very bad for the giraffe and the zebra, for he would lie down by a yellow stone or a clump of grass, and when one of them came by, he would surprise them out of their lives.

An **Ethiopian** also lived on the High Veldt with the leopard. The two hunted together—the Ethiopian with his bows and arrows, the leopard with his teeth and claws—till the giraffe, the zebra and the other animals didn't know which way to run. After some time, they learned to avoid anything that looked like a leopard or an Ethiopian; and went away from the High Veldt.

They came to a great forest, full of trees and bushes and stripy, **speckly**, patchy shadows, and there they hid. After some time, the giraffe grew **blotchy**, and the zebra grew stripy. So, though you could hear and smell them, you could rarely see them, they were so well camouflaged now.

Did You Know? Science

Camouflage is the way in which an animal's colour or shape matches with its surroundings, making it difficult to find it. Most animals have this ability. It increases their chances of survival by helping them hide from animals which hunt them.

Meanwhile, the leopard and the Ethiopian ran about, wondering where their breakfasts and dinners had gone. They went for advice to Baviaan, the dog-headed, barking baboon, the wisest animal in all of southern Africa.

Who was the wisest animal in southern Africa?

'Where has all the **game** gone?' they asked.

Baviaan winked. He knew. 'The game has gone to other spots. My advice to you is to go into other spots as soon as you can.'

This **puzzled** the leopard and the Ethiopian. They set off to look for game. After many days, they saw a tall forest full of tree trunks.

'What is this?' said the leopard, 'It is so dark, yet so full of little pieces of light.'

game: (here) wild animals hunted for food

puzzled: confused

knocked down: hit someone and made them fall to the ground

scramble: quick movement with some difficulty

chestnut: brown-coloured

'I can smell the giraffe and I can hear him, but I can't see him,' said the Ethiopian.

'I suppose it is because we have just come in from the sunshine,' said the leopard.

'It's a long time since we hunted them. Perhaps we have forgotten what they look like.'

'Nonsense!' said the leopard. 'I remember them perfectly. The giraffe is about seventeen feet high, golden-yellow from head to heel. The zebra is about four and a half feet high and of a grey colour.'

The leopard and the Ethiopian searched all day, but they could not find any of them. They decided to wait until dark. Then the leopard heard someone sniffing. In the starlight, it seemed to have stripes and it smelt like the zebra. When he **knocked** it **down**, it kicked like the zebra too. Soon, he heard a grunt, a crash and a **scramble**.

The Ethiopian called out, 'I have caught a thing that I can't see. But it smells and kicks like the giraffe.'

'Don't you trust it,' said the leopard. 'Sit on its head till the morning—same as me.'

So they sat on the zebra and the giraffe. In the morning, the leopard asked, 'What do you have?'

The Ethiopian scratched his head and said, 'It should be the giraffe; but it is covered with **chestnut** blotches. What about you?'

The leopard replied, 'It ought to be the zebra; but it is covered all over with black and purple stripes. What in the world have you been doing to yourself, zebra? Don't you know that if you were on the High Veldt I could see you ten miles away?'

'But this isn't the High Veldt,' the zebra replied. 'Can't you see?'

'I can now,' said the leopard. 'How is it done?'

'Let us get up,' said the zebra, 'and we will show you.'

They let the zebra and the giraffe get up. The zebra moved away to some thorn bushes where the sunlight fell in stripes. The giraffe moved off to some tallish trees where the shadows were all blotchy.

'Now watch,' they said. 'This is the way it's done. One—two—three! And where's your breakfast?'

The leopard and the Ethiopian **stared**, but all they could see were the shadows in the forest. The zebra and giraffe had just walked off and hidden themselves in the shadowy forest.

'Hey!' said the Ethiopian. 'That's a trick worth learning. I'm going to take Baviaan's advice. He told me I ought to change.'

'What to?' asked the leopard, excited.

'To a dark colour. It will help me hide in **hollows** and behind trees.'

How would the dark colour help the Ethiopian?

stared: looked for a long time

hollows: holes

The Ethiopian changed his skin then and there.

'Baviaan's told you to go into spots too,' he told the leopard.

'I did,' said the leopard. 'I went into other spots as fast as I could.'

'Oh,' said the Ethiopian, 'Baviaan didn't mean spots in Africa. He meant spots on your skin.'

'What's the use of that?' said the leopard.

'Think of what the giraffe and the zebra did,' said the Ethiopian. 'I don't want to go hunting without you, but I must if you keep looking like a sunflower against a dark fence.'

'I'll take spots, then,' said the leopard.

'I'll make them with the tips of my fingers,' said the Ethiopian.

So, he put his five fingers close together and pressed them all over the leopard. Wherever his fingers touched, they left five little black marks, close together. You can see them on the leopard's skin even today.

'Now you are a beauty!' said the Ethiopian. 'You can lie on the bare ground and look like a heap of pebbles. You can lie on a leafy branch and look like sunshine passing through the leaves. Think of that and purr!'

So, they went away and lived happily. Since that time, the leopard has always had his spots.

Who looked like a beauty after getting spots?

About the author

Rudyard Kipling (1865–1936) is one of the most popular English writers. He was born in pre-independence India. *The Jungle Book* and *Kim*, both set in India, are some of his best-loved books for children.

Comprehension

Quick Recap

A. Answer the questions in a few lines.

1. Describe the High Veldt.
2. Why was the sandy colour of the leopard bad for the giraffe and the zebra?
3. How did the Ethiopian and the leopard hunt?
4. Who did the Ethiopian and the leopard go to for advice and why?
5. How did the zebra and the giraffe escape after being caught by the leopard and the Ethiopian?
6. What did the Ethiopian decide to change to and why?
7. How did the Ethiopian make spots on the leopard's skin?
8. According to the Ethiopian, how could the leopard blend with his surroundings with his new spots?

B. Read the lines from the story and answer the questions.

1. *'What is this? It is so dark, yet so full of little pieces of light.'*
   a. Who said these words and to whom?
   b. What was the speaker describing?
   c. Why had they come to that place?

2. *'I'll make them with the tips of my fingers,'*
   a. Who said these words and to whom?
   b. What was the speaker going to make?
   c. Why did the listener need 'them' on its body?

Life Skills and Values

collaboration and team work

Think and answer.

1. How did the giraffe and the zebra overcome the problems that they faced in the High Veldt?
2. When Baviaan advised the leopard and Ethiopian to 'go look into other spots', what did he mean? What did the leopard think he had meant?

Way with Words

A. Write the nationalities for the following countries. One is done for you.

1. *A citizen of Ethiopia:* *Ethiopian*
2. A citizen of Australia: ______________
3. A citizen of Nepal: ______________
4. A citizen of Sri Lanka: ______________
5. A citizen of England: ______________
6. A citizen of France: ______________
7. A citizen of Japan: ______________
8. A citizen of Pakistan: ______________

Suffixes

You have studied that a suffix is a group of letters added after a word to form a new word.
Example: The friend**ship** between the man the leopard was unique. (friend+**ship**)

B. Complete the suffix wheels. The words around each central circle should form complete words when added to the suffix at the centre. One is done for you.

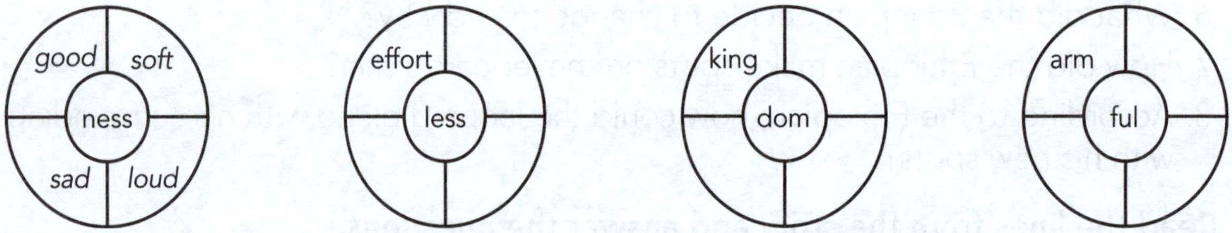

Grammar in Use

Adjective Phrase

An **adjective phrase** is a group of words that function as an adjective.

Look at the sentence.

The forest was full of **patchy** shadows.

This sentence can be rewritten as:

The forest was full of shadows **with patches.**

The adjective, 'patchy' in the first sentence is being replaced in the second sentence by the adjective phrase, 'with patches'.

A. Write an adjective for each of these adjective phrases.

1. made of gold ________
2. having great wealth ________
3. of great beauty ________
4. full of anger ________
5. of great taste ________
6. of great learning ________

B. Complete the following sentences using these adjective phrases.

cut into cubes	made of satin	covered with mud
decorated with rubies	made with a lot of spices	
with white lace around the collar		

1. At the party, Ravi had a curry ____________________.
2. The crown was ____________________.
3. Raj finally decided to buy the sheets ____________________.
4. The boy was ____________________ after the football game.
5. I love to eat mangoes ____________________.
6. Ria bought the shirt ____________________.

Study Skills

Spell Check

The letters, **oo** and **ue** often have the same pronunciation.

Examples: zoo true

Complete the words using either oo or ue.

1. cl____ 2. bl____ 3. t____th 4. f____l 5. gl____
6. bab____n 7. h____t 8. b____t 9. sm____th 10. st____l

Listening and Speaking

Listen to a conversation in which Baavian gives advice to the Ethiopian. Then, offer your advice on each of the following situations.

Situation 1:

Ravi: There is nobody at home and I am really hungry. What do I do?

Situation 2:

Priya: I saw a rat near my bookshelf yesterday and I fear that it might destroy my books. What should I do?

Situation 3:

Mr Roy: There are so many clothes in my cupboard that don't fit me anymore. What do I do with them?

Pen it Down

21st Century Information Literacy

Find out the following details for five animals that use camouflage to defend themselves.

- name of the animal
- where it is found
- two features of the animal
- how it uses camouflage

Then, write a short paragraph about each animal using these points. You could also include a picture of each animal camouflaged in its surroundings.

Self Assessment

Now I can

- read and understand a story on how all living creatures adapt and adjust to new surroundings.
- use suffixes, identify adjective phrases and spell words with *oo* and *ue*.
- offer advice on various situations and write short paragraphs on animals.

Read More

The Jungle Book: This book by Rudyard Kipling is about the life and adventures of Mowgli, a child who is raised by a family of wolves in the forest.

In Bon Bibi's Forest: This book by Sandhya Rao is about a monster, who lives in the forest, and its protector, Bon Bibi. It is based on the idea of peace between humans and animals.

16

The Girl Who Stepped on the Loaf

Augusta Stevenson

Let's Get Started

Christmas, like most festivals, is a time for sharing and celebration. There are many traditions associated with this festival. Look at the pictures and identify the Christmas traditions practised across the world. Use the phrases given in the help box.

play on the birth of Jesus	making gingerbread houses	singing carols
decorating Christmas trees	meeting Santa	exchanging gifts

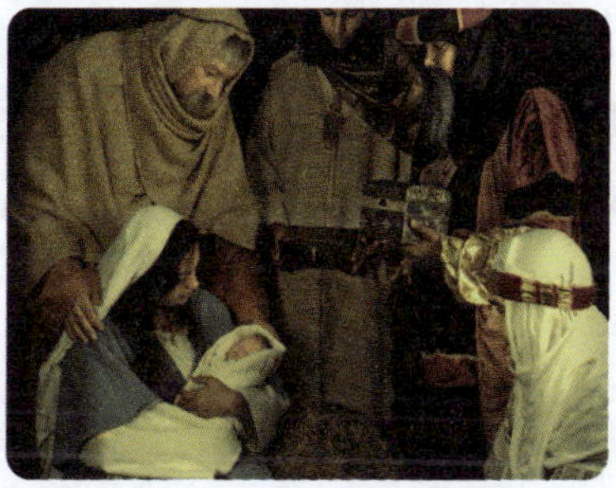

Active Participation: Joy of participation in the collective

Reading

Have you ever gone against your parents' wishes when they asked you not to do something? What was the result? Inge does not listen to her mother and gets into trouble. Read this play to find out how she gets out of the tricky situation.

Characters

Inge
Her mother
Wicked elf
The sparrow
The peasant
Gretel
First stone
Second stone
Third stone
The very old sparrow
The old sparrow
The young sparrow
The very young sparrow

Did You Know? G.K.

Elves are thought to be magical creatures who could use their powers both for helping and harming people.

Scene I

The day before Christmas. Inge's mother's home.

Mother stands at the kitchen window, waiting for Inge.

Which day was it?

Mother Ah, here she comes at last!
(*Enter Inge*) I have waited long for you, my child. Where have you been?
(*Inge is silent*) Have you been to the Elf Hill again? Tell me.

hesitating: being slow to act

indignantly: angrily

Inge (**hesitating**) Just for a little while, mother.

Mother Inge! Inge! What have I always told you?

Inge I thought I'd go just this once.

Mother (*sadly*) Ah, Inge, that's what you always say.

Inge There's no harm talking with the elves.

Mother And I, your mother, say there is harm.

Inge But, mother,—they talk so prettily.

Mother (*nodding*) Aye! and that's the harm. They've put such silly ideas into your head.

Inge They say it is friendship that makes them talk as they do.

Mother (**indignantly**) Friendship! It is friendship, is it, to tell you not to fetch the wood?

Inge They say it will spoil my hands.

Mother Out upon them and their pretty talk! You shall go there no more. Do you hear me, Inge?

Inge (**pouting**) I hear.

Mother Now take this loaf of bread to your sick aunt. Say to her that it is her Christmas gift.

Inge But, mother, I must cross the muddy road to go there.

Mother Well, you are neither sugar nor salt.

Inge I'll spoil my shoes!

Mother You think of your shoes while your aunt lies ill?

What did Inge's mother give her to take to her aunt?

Inge Wait till spring and the mud will be gone.

Mother Wait till spring and your aunt will be gone! Here is the loaf—now off with you!

Inge takes the loaf and goes but not ***willingly****.*

Scene II

A few minutes later. The muddy road.

Inge stops at the muddy road.

Inge It is too wide to leap!

The Wicked elf appears on the opposite side of the road.

Wicked elf Good day to you, pretty maid!

Inge Good day to you, dear Elf!

Wicked elf Will you cross this muddy road?

Inge I must.

Wicked elf Then I'll tell you how to do it and not so much as wet your shoe.

Inge Oh, thank you, dear Elf!

Wicked elf Throw down your loaf and—use it as a **stepping stone**.

Inge But it will spoil the bread!

Wicked elf But it will save your shoes!

Inge Well, that's true—

Wordwise

The phrase 'neither sugar nor salt' is used to refer to somebody who does not want to go out in the rain. It borrows from the idea that both sugar and salt dissolve in water.

pouting: (here) pushing out the lips when upset
willingly: cheerfully
stepping stone: a raised stone to step on when crossing a stream

Why didn't Inge want to go across the muddy road?

fastened: attached

drawing: (here) pulling

brook: a narrow river

Wicked elf A pretty maid never wears a muddy shoe. Come, throw down the loaf!

Inge Well, I'll do it!

She throws the loaf and steps upon it. It is sinking! What shall I do?

Wicked elf Why, then, jump off!

Inge (*trying to jump*) I can't! Don't you see I can't?

Wicked elf Ha, ha! You're **fastened** to it!

Inge It is **drawing** me down! Help me! Help me!

Wicked elf There's no help for you. You must go down with the loaf.

Inge Please save me! See how I'm sinking! The mud will soon be over my shoes!

Wicked elf The mud will soon be over your head! Do you wish to be saved by magic?

Inge Yes, yes!

Wicked elf Listen, then—I'll change you into a bird. Are you willing?

Inge Yes! Quick now, before I sink deeper!

Wicked elf (*nodding its head thrice*) A sparrow shall you be! Change, now change!

Inge changes into a sparrow, with a tuft of white feathers in the shape of a loaf of bread upon its head. The sparrow flies away from the mud.

Sparrow Now change me back into Inge.

Wicked elf You shall remain as you are until you can change yourself back.

Sparrow And when will that be?

Wicked elf When the loaf has gone from your head.

Sparrow The loaf from my head? What do you mean?

Wicked elf (*going*) Fly away to the **brook** and see! Ha, ha, ha!

What did the elf change Inge to?

Scene III

The day following Christmas Day. An old stone wall by a brook.

The sparrow sits in a hole in the wall.

First stone Come, come, don't be so sad, little sparrow!

Second stone Come, lift up your head and sing!

Third stone Come, sing us your Christmas song!

Sparrow Sing! I have nothing to sing about.

First stone Sing of your friends.

Second stone Sing of their love for you.

Third stone Sing of their kindness to you.

Sparrow Talk not to me of friends or love or kindness! There's none in the world.

Enter a peasant with his little daughter, Gretel. The peasant carries two ears of corn.

Peasant Now, my Gretel, we'll place the corn here on the old wall.

Gretel Mother thought you brought too much.

Peasant Well, it is true that there are only three ears left at home, but the birds must have their Christmas dinner.

He places the corn on the wall.

Gretel There's none about to see it!

What was the name of the peasant's daughter?

Peasant Oh, some bird will soon find it!

Gretel But will it call the others?

Peasant We'll wait to see. Come, we'll sit on the log.

They go to a log nearby.

First stone There, little sparrow, can you say now there is no kindness?

Second stone Or love?

Third stone Or friendship?

Sparrow No, no! I can never say that again. The peasant's heart is full of kindness and love and friendship. I will sing of it! It will be my Christmas song!

The sparrow leaves the hole and flies to the corn.

Gretel Look, father, there is a sparrow! And hear it sing! Just hear it!

Peasant It is calling the other birds.

Gretel Why, it doesn't even touch the corn!

Peasant It's waiting to share it with the others. Is it not a pretty sight? Come, we must go and tell mother.

Scene IV

One month later.

All the sparrows except our sparrow sit on the stone wall.

What did the peasant and his daughter see?

Young sparrow I say the stranger should be driven away!

Very young sparrow So say I!

Old sparrow The stranger is a sparrow, but still not a sparrow.

Very old sparrow And yet she is only different by a tuft of white feathers.

Young sparrow And such a tuft! For all the world like a loaf of bread!

Very young sparrow I'd think it is a shame to carry such a thing on one's head!

Old sparrow I fear it will shame us all to have this stranger around us.

Very old sparrow And yet we are not ashamed to eat the crumbs this stranger brings.

Old sparrow Well, it is true that she has been most kind.

Very old sparrow It is a hard winter! Shall we drive away the one who finds food where we find none?

Young sparrow And calls us every time!

Very young sparrow And never eats till we have come!

crumbs: very small pieces of food

Very old sparrow I've kept in mind the **crumbs** she has found us. How many do you think?

Old sparrow I cannot say, for I did not think to notice.

Very old sparrow It only needs two or three crumbs now to make a complete loaf.

Other sparrows (*greatly surprised*) A loaf?

Very old sparrow (*nodding*) A loaf.

Very young sparrow Here comes the stranger now!

Old sparrow She brings a crust!

Our sparrow flies up with a crust in its bill.

Sparrow Come, friends, it is for all of you!

Very old sparrow Do you know, stranger bird, that, with these crumbs, you have brought us in all one loaf?

Our sparrow drops the crust for the others. At once it changes into Inge. The birds fly away in fear.

Inge Ah! Now I understand. The loaf had to be made up, crumb by crumb.

The wicked elf suddenly appears.

Wicked elf Come, pretty maid, come to the Elf Hill!

Inge No, no! I will not!

Wicked elf But we have such pretty things to tell you!

Inge I do not care for your pretty things! I will fetch wood for my mother. I will walk in the mud if need be. I'll have nothing to do with you! Away, away, I say!

About the author

Augusta Stevenson (1872–1976) was a teacher and a children's writer. She wrote over 400 children's books, her most famous books being *Childhood of Famous Americans* and *Children's Classics in Dramatic Form.*

Comprehension

Quick Recap

A. Answer the questions in a few lines.

1. Why did Mother ask Inge not to go to the Elf Hill?
2. What task did Mother ask Inge to do? What was her response?
3. What did the elf ask Inge to do to prevent her shoes from getting muddy?
4. How did the elf trick Inge when she was sinking?

5. For whom did the peasant bring corn, and why?
6. What did the sparrow decide after seeing the peasant's actions?
7. What did the young sparrows want to do to the sparrow? Why?
8. Why did the very old sparrow say it was wrong to drive the sparrow away?
9. How did Inge change back to her original self?

B. Read the lines from the story and answer the questions.

1. *'They say it will spoil my hands.'*
   a. Who said these words?
   b. Who does 'they' refer to? Where did they live?
   c. What would spoil the speaker's hands?

2. *'Well, it is true that she has been most kind.'*
   a. Who said these words?
   b. Who does 'she' refer to?
   c. How did 'she' show her kindness?

Life Skills and Values kindness, sharing with others

Think and answer.

1. Why do you think that the elf put wicked ideas into Inge's head?
2. What quality in Inge made her help the other sparrows?
3. What lesson did Inge learn at the end of the play?

Way with Words

A. Complete the sentences using the following movement verbs.

crawled	leapt	slithered	galloped	walked	jumped

1. The snake _______________ across the path and disappeared into the bushes.
2. The thief _______________ over the wall and ran away quickly.
3. The frog _______________ from the stone into the pond.
4. Rani _______________ along the river bank.
5. The baby _______________ across the carpet towards the toy.
6. The horse _______________ across the meadow with John on its back.

B. Read the clues and complete this crossword on words related to magic.

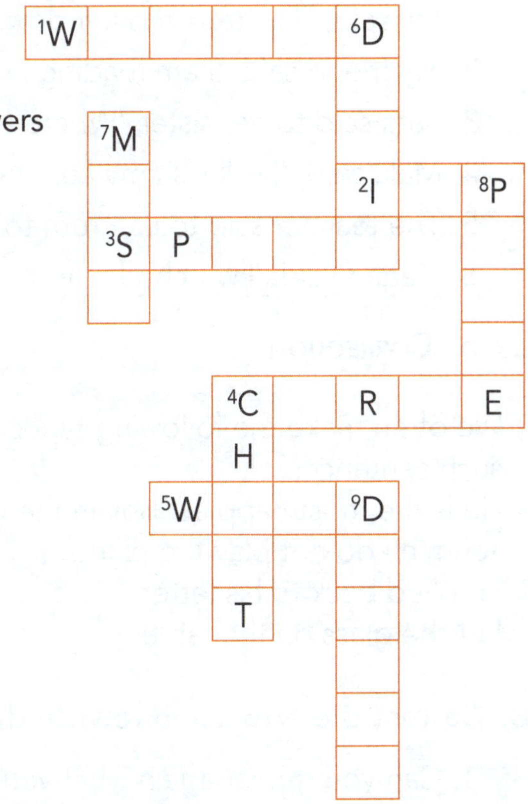

Across:

1. a man with magical powers
2. a small mischievous creature with magical powers
3. words with magical powers
4. words used to harm someone
5. stick used by a magician

Down:

4. say something repeatedly
6. the most powerful evil spirit
7. a covering for the face
8. a supernatural creature with pointed ears
9. a monster that breathes fire

Grammar in Use

Direct and Indirect Speech

When we write the exact words of the speaker in a sentence, it is said to be in **direct speech**. The words of the speaker are placed between inverted commas (' ').

Example: Mother said to Inge, 'Now take this loaf of bread to your sick aunt.'

When we report what the speaker has said, it is said to be in **indirect speech**.

Example: Mother asked Inge to take the loaf of bread to her sick aunt.

Remember the following rules when you rewrite a sentence in indirect speech.

Indirect speech

- First and second person pronouns (*I*, *we*, *you*, etc) change to third person pronouns (*he*, *she*, *it*, *they*, etc).
  Example: The Sparrow said, '**I** will sing of it.' (direct speech)
  The Sparrow said that **she** would sing of it.' (indirect speech)
- The present tense changes to the past tense.
  Example: Mother **asked** Inge to take the loaf of bread to her sick aunt.
- Inverted commas are not used in indirect speech.
  Example: He said that he would return.

A. Rewrite the sentences in indirect speech.

1. Raj said, 'The tree was cut down yesterday.'
2. My friend said, 'I am reading an interesting book.'
3. Sara said to her sister, 'Where are you going now?'
4. Mala said, 'I will visit my aunt next month.'
5. The teacher said to us, 'Turn to page sixty-two.'
6. Gagan said, 'I watched a horror film last week.'

Error Correction

We often make the following types of errors in English. Look at the correct usage for such sentences.

He is the most happiest boy in the world.	[✗]	He is the happiest boy in the world.	[✓]
Tehmina do not play the piano.	[✗]	Tehmina does not play the piano.	[✓]
I replied back to his letter.	[✗]	I replied to his letter.	[✓]
Put the glass on the table.	[✗]	Keep the glass on the table.	[✓]

B. Correct the errors and rewrite the sentences.

1. Can you repeat again what you just said?
2. Raj did a lot of mistakes in his composition.
3. My most favourite author is Ruskin Bond.
4. Mr Roy has a black expensive wallet.
5. The boy returned back from school at six in the evening.
6. When did you came here?

Study Skills

Use Your Dictionary

Write the meanings of the compound words using your dictionary in your notebook. Mention the headword in the dictionary under which you found each word.

1. lukewarm	3. fortnight	5. backdrop	7. forearm
2. underage	4. keyhole	6. deadline	8. cartwheel

Listening and Speaking

Listen to a conversation between a crocodile and a rabbit. What do you think the theme of the conversation is? Discuss the theme in groups of four and talk about it in your class.

Pen it Down

You are walking down an empty street on a Sunday afternoon when you bump into someone. You look up and see a beautiful lady. She says that she is a fairy and that she would grant you three wishes because you have been a good person.

Write a dialogue on your conversation with the fairy. You should also mention what wishes you would ask for and why.

HC Identifying needs of the self

Self Assessment

Now I can

- read and understand a play about why we should always listen to the advice of elders.
- practise movement verbs and complete a crossword on words related to magic.
- change sentences from direct to indirect speech and correct errors in sentences.
- discuss the theme of a conversation and write a dialogue.

Read More

Araminta Spookie, My Haunted House: This book by Angie Sage is about a girl, Araminta, who lives in a haunted house, and her plot to stop her home from being sold.

Rumplestiltskin: This story by the Grimm Brothers is about a miller's daughter who takes the help of the magical creature Rumpelstiltskin to spin straw into gold. In return, he asks her to give him her first child when the king marries her.

light verse

17

Humour

My Elephant is Missing

Kenn Nesbitt

SUSTAINABLE DEVELOPMENT GOALS 15

Let's Get Started

Match the following to learn more about elephants.

Column A	Column B
1. Elephants are	a. the age of 60 in the wild.
2. There are two species of	b. peanut, shell it, remove the shell and eat the nut.
3. Elephants can live till	c. the world's largest land animal.
4. Elephants can pick up a	d. suck up water to drink.
5. Elephants use their trunks to	e. tusks, made of ivory.
6. They have been killed for their	f. elephants: African and Asian.

HC **Active Participation:** Recognizing characteristics and intrinsic nature of entities

Reading

Have you ever lost anything? Where did you go looking for it? Humans and elephants

have shared a special relationship since ancient times. Read this poem about a boy and his elephant.

I cannot find my elephant.
He must have run away.
He isn't on the sofa
where he promised he would stay.

I've looked around the living room,
the kitchen and the hall.
My elephant is missing
and I'm not sure who to call.

I'll need to get a **bloodhound**
who can **track** him by his scent,
or hire a house **detective**
to discover where he went.

He isn't in the basement
or the **attic** or the **yard**.
You'd think, to find an elephant
would not be quite so hard.

Perhaps I'll make some posters,
and I'll offer a reward.
I'd make it more, but fifty **cents**
is all I can **afford**.

If you should see my elephant,
he answers to 'Jerome.'
Please tell him that I miss him
and I wish he'd come back home.

He knows the way. It's up the street
and down our garden path.
And next time I won't warn him
when it's time to take his bath.

Where did the elephant promise he would stay?

bloodhound: a large dog with a good sense of smell

track: find somebody by following the marks or signs they have left

detective: a person who solves crimes and catches criminals

attic: a room or space just below the roof of a house, used for storing things

yard: garden or an area outside a building

cents: coins; unit of money in many countries, like the US

afford: have enough money to buy something

About the poet

Kenn Nesbitt (1962–) lives in Washington, USA. Some of his collections of poems for children are *My Hippo Has the Hiccups* and *The Biggest Burp Ever.*

Comprehension

Quick Recap

A. Complete this passage about the poem.

The speaker is worried because he cannot ____________ his elephant. The speaker has checked the ____________, in the living room, ____________ and the ____________. But the ____________ is missing. The speaker thinks he should get a ____________ to find him by his scent, or, hire a house ____________ to track him down. It is not easy to ____________ an ____________.

B. Answer these questions in a few lines.

1. Where did the speaker look for the missing elephant?
2. Who can track the elephant by its scent?
3. What does the speaker want to offer someone who finds the elephant?
4. What is the name of the elephant?
5. Does the speaker love his elephant? Which lines in the poem tell you so?

Life Skills and Values imagination, creativity

Think and answer.

1. Why do you think the elephant ran away?
2. Do you think the elephant will come back home? Why?
3. Do you think the elephant in the poem is a real animal or is it a toy? Give reasons for your answer.

21ST CENTURY Critical Thinking

Way with Words

Rhyming Words

A. Look at these rhyming words from the poem. Add a rhyming word to each list.

1. away, stay ____________
2. hall, call ____________
3. scent, went ____________
4. yard, hard ____________
5. reward, afford ____________
6. path, bath ____________

Homophones

The words **scent** and **cent** have the same pronunciation but different spellings and meanings. Such words are **homophones**.

B. Complete the sentences with the correct homophones. Look up the meanings of the words in a dictionary if required.

1. My aunt lit the incense stick and the ______________ (scent/cent) filled the room.
2. My school fees is ______________ (due/dew) in three days.
3. Please give me a ______________ (peace/piece) of chalk.
4. We should not ______________ (waste/waist) water.
5. We had nothing to do, so we were ______________. (bored/board)
6. Sonia ______________ (through/threw) away her torn shoes.
7. The ______________ can ______________ seen hovering on the flowers to collect nectar. (be/bee)
8. The ______________ of the ship is not on ______________. (sale/sail)

Grammar in Use

Apostrophe: Contractions

You know that a **contraction** is a word formed by joining two or more words and leaving out some letters. We use an apostrophe in contractions to show where the letters have been dropped. Look at the given table.

Words	Contractions
I will	I'll
I have	I've
I would	I'd
it is	it's
will not	won't

In the contraction **I'll**, the apostrophe indicates that the letters **wi** are missing, while in **I've**, the apostrophe shows that the letters **ha** are missing. Contractions are usually used in spoken English.

A. Write the contractions of these words.

1. you would ______________
2. you have ______________
3. is not ______________
4. does not ______________
5. he will ______________
6. cannot ______________
7. I would ______________
8. who is ______________

B. Rewrite these sentences using contractions.

1. I will go to bed early as I have school tomorrow.
2. Do not play with fire.
3. I am playing chess with my cousin.
4. I will not throw stones at stray dogs.
5. They will visit their aunt in Mumbai next month.
6. He does not keep the tap running while taking a bath.

Study Skills

Pronounce Well

Read each word list. Underline the word which sounds different in each set.

1. but, hut, put, nut, cut
2. rear, bear, dear, fear, near
3. sow, low, bow, now, row

Listening and Speaking

Listen to the poem 'Never Touched an Elephant' by Meg Wiseman. Your teacher will play it twice. Note down the words related to touch. Check the list by comparing it with your partner's.

Pen it Down

You have lost an expensive watch that your father gifted you on your birthday. You are very upset. Your teacher has allowed you to put up a notice on the school notice board about the lost watch.

Write a notice requesting the students of your school to help you find the lost watch.

You can include the following points:

- description of the watch
- place where you think you lost it
- your contact number
- the reward for the person who finds it

Self Assessment

Now I can

- read and understand a funny poem about a boy and his pet elephant.
- use rhyming words and homophones.
- use the apostrophe for contractions, and write a notice.

Read More

The Secret Place: This poem by Dorothy Aldis talks about the narrator's favourite place in a tree where she likes to hide.

My Shadow: This poem for children by Robert Louis Stevenson is about the relationship a young child shares with his shadow.

18

Harriet and the Underground Railroad

Philip Steele

Let's Get Started

During the coronavirus pandemic, which struck in March 2020, many of us stayed at home most of the time. Simple things, like playing with friends in the park, or going to busy markets with parents, were not possible.

Complete the table comparing things that changed during the lockdown. You could include the following topics: going to school, playing with friends, travelling on holiday.

During Lockdown	Before Lockdown

HC Feelings: Taking responsibility in conflicts

Reading

Harriet Tubman was born a slave in America. Find out how she escaped and led other slaves to freedom.

It was a cold winter day in Maryland, USA, in 1828. Six-year-old Minty was checking **muskrat** traps along the

muskrat: a North American creature bigger than a rat that destroys crops river for a local white man, to whom she had been hired out. It was cold and dangerous work, unfit for a child. Minty was down with measles but had to keep working. Often, she was so sick that her mother had to beg for her to be brought home until she got better.

Minty, or Araminta Harriet Ross, was a slave. She was owned by a white family and could be bought or sold at any time, just like her parents, who were also slaves.

Minty's troubles

Soon after, Minty went to work for a **bad-tempered** woman called Miss Susan. Minty had to clean her house and rock the baby's cradle. After hours on duty, Minty sometimes fell asleep. If the baby woke up crying after the rocking stopped, Minty was **whipped**.

Once, Minty was caught taking a lump of sugar from the kitchen. She was so afraid of being punished that she ran away and hid with some animals in a nearby farm for five days. She survived on **scraps** fed to them. When she returned, terribly hungry, she was badly whipped. The scars on her back would stay forever.

Such a life was only too common for slaves. They often worked long hours, without any pay, and were forced to live in **rundown** and overcrowded wooden **cabins**.

bad-tempered: someone who is angry and rude most of the time

whipped: beaten with a belt, stick or rod

scraps: leftover food

rundown: poor or bad state

cabins: (here) small, single-storey houses

plantation: (here) large areas of land, where cotton, sugarcane and other crops are grown

visions: dreams or similar experiences, sometimes of a religious kind

Growing up as a slave

Minty's father worked on a **plantation**, chopping wood while her mother was a cook. When Minty was just two years old, she and her eight brothers and sisters were forced to move with their mother to another property 15 km away, leaving their father behind.

When Minty was about 13 years old, she had an accident that changed her life. On her way to a store, she saw a landowner arguing with a young runaway slave. The white man threw a heavy iron weight at the boy, hitting Minty instead. She was badly injured. For the rest of her life, she had headaches and powerful **visions** which she believed were messages from God giving her the courage to act.

Escape to freedom

Slavery was slowly **banned** in the northern states of America. Many slaves began escaping to the free states along secret roads nicknamed the 'Underground Railroad'.

They travelled on horses, carts or boats. They hid in caves, country barns, and the **cellars** of safe houses, helped by white people who were against slavery and free Black people.

banned: stopped officially

cellar: a room underneath a building that is used to store things

crooned: sang

These people led slaves to the next 'station'. No one knew who ran the other stations. That way, it was safer.

When Harriet, as she was now known, was about 27, she was to be sold off after her owner's death, as payment for his debts. All slaves feared being sold. A new owner could be crueller and work conditions much harder. Harriet remembered her sisters being sold, and how her mother had hidden her brother, Moses, when a man came to buy him.

Harriet decided to join the Underground Railroad with two of her younger brothers. After a failed try, she again made plans to set off northwards, on her own.

Before leaving, Harriet went to say goodbye to her mother. There were too many people around, so she could only sing a well-known song as a secret message. She **crooned**: *Farewell, oh farewell, I'll meet you in the morning,*
I'm bound for the promised land.

What was the nickname given to the secret roads?

Harriet travelled 150 kilometres, following back routes through **swamps** and woods. At every moment, she watched out for **slave catchers**. She learnt to travel by night or hide under goods on the back of **wagons**.

When she finally reached the state of Pennsylvania, where there was no slavery, she felt like she had arrived in heaven!

Working on the Underground Railroad

Harriet found work cooking and serving in hotels in Pennsylvania's capital city, Philadelphia. In 1850, she returned to Maryland on a **daring** mission to rescue her niece Kessiah, and Kessiah's two children, who were to be sold.

On the day of the **auction**, someone made a bid for Kessiah and the children. By the time the auctioneers realised that the bid was false, the slaves had escaped on a boat, sailing to the city of Baltimore. From there, Harriet guided them to Philadelphia.

In the next ten years, Harriet made 13 trips south to rescue slaves. She hid in people's backyards, slept in snowy woods and wore **disguises**. To avoid being caught, she said that she was travelling south instead of north.

Wordwise

The word 'Black' refers to the darker skin colour of people whose forefathers were slaves from Africa. Many 'Black' Americans use the term, 'African Americans' today. It is thought to be more respectful as it describes who they are instead of their skin colour.

Who did Harriet watch out for?

swamps: water-covered areas in which plants and trees grow

slave catchers: people who were paid to catch and bring back runaway slaves

wagons: vehicles with four wheels that were pulled by horses, used for carrying heavy goods

daring: brave

auction: a public sale where things (here people) are sold to the buyer who can pay the highest price

disguises: something that you wear to change how you look so that people don't recognize you

In 1850, a law was passed to let slave catchers work in northern states as well. Slaves were no longer safe until they crossed into the neighbouring country of Canada. In 1857, when her father was accused of helping slaves escape, Harriet led both her parents there. She would help free around 70 people.

Harriet goes to war

In 1861, the American Civil War began between the northern and southern states of America. Harriet joined the war, working as a **spy** to help find enemy soldiers. That year, she took part in an armed **raid**, with 300 troops. Over 700 slaves joined them, escaping from their plantations.

The southern states were defeated after a terrible, four-year struggle and slavery was **abolished** throughout America. But Black people's struggle for **equality** was far from over. While returning from the war, Harriet's arm was injured by railroad officers on a train, who refused to accept her US Army papers. They didn't believe that slaves could have the same rights as them.

Did You Know? History

The American Civil War, from 1861 to 1865, was fought between the northern and the southern states. The war started because the south refused to stop slavery, which was a big source of its wealth.

spy: someone who finds out secret information about another country or group

raid: a quick surprise attack

abolished: put an end to a system through a law

equality: equal rights for all

boast: something that you speak about proudly

Soon laws were passed to make it hard for Black people to have the full rights of American citizens. But Harriet never gave up fighting. In the 1890s, she spoke out for all women to be given the right to vote.

Harriet died peacefully on 10 March 1913 in a care home she founded for old people. To the end, she told stories of the days of slavery. Her proudest **boast** was, 'I was a conductor on the Underground Railroad for eight years ... I never ran my train off the track and I never lost a passenger.'

Comprehension

Quick Recap

A. Answer these questions.

1. What work did Minty do for Miss Susan?
2. Why did Minty run away to a nearby farm? How did she live there?
3. Which accident changed Minty's life?
4. Why did Harriet go back to Maryland in 1850?
5. What work did Harriet do in the war?
6. What was the 'Underground Railroad'? Why did Harriet join it?

B. Read the lines from the passage and answer the questions.

1. *Six-year-old Minty was checking muskrat traps along the river*
   a. Where was Minty? What was her full name?
   b. Why was she checking muskrat traps?
   c. How was Minty's health at that time?
2. *'Farewell, oh farewell, I'll meet you in the morning, I'm bound for the promised land.'*
   a. Who sang this song and for whom?
   b. Why did the person sing and not speak these lines?
   c. What was she trying to say through the song?

Life Skills and Values — selflessness, courage

Think and answer.

1. What kind of a person was Harriet? Write down two of her qualities. Give an example explaining each quality.
2. Write four sentences describing the life of a slave in America in Harriet's time.

Way with Words

Idioms with Catch

An **idiom** is a group of words which has a meaning which is different from the meaning of each word that it is made of.

Example: I'm **bound for** the promised land. (bound for = moving towards a particular place)

A. Match these idioms that use the word 'catch' with their meanings.

Idiom	Meaning
1. catch on	a. rest for a moment while doing something tiring
2. catch you later	b. start burning
3. catch your breath	c. get someone's attention
4. catch a cold	d. understand what is being said
5. catch fire	e. get a runny nose and possibly, even fever
6. catch someone's eye	f. a way of saying goodbye

Collocations: Verbs and Nouns

B. Choose the correct pair of verbs and nouns from the box to complete the following sentences.

buy, laptop	goes, classes	catch, cold
misses, bus	rows, boat	have, dream

1. The sailor ____________ the ____________ gently down the stream.
2. My sister ____________ for painting ____________ every week.
3. You will ____________ a ____________ if you don't change your wet clothes.
4. Jaya never ____________ the ____________ to school.
5. I ____________ a ____________ of visiting Disneyland some day.
6. Dilip will ____________ a ____________ for his brother.

Grammar in Use

Subject-verb Agreement

You know that the verb in a sentence must agree with its subject in number and person. Look at the sentences.

Each of Harriet's trips is a dangerous one.

Every slave was exploited by her owner.

The words **each** and **every** are always followed by a singular verb. Here, the verbs are **is** and **was** respectively.

A. Underline the correct verbs.

1. Each of the students was/were intelligent.
2. Every book was/were kept neatly on the table.
3. Seema and her sister has/have a pet cat and a dog.
4. She follows/follow all the rules in school.
5. There is/are many children in the pool.
6. Every student was/were sitting silently in the library.
7. Mathematics is/are my favourite subject.

Conjunctions

Conjunctions are words that link other words, and phrases together.

Read the following sentences.

It was cold **and** dangerous work, unfit for a child.

The conjunction **and** joins the two adjectives 'cold' and 'dangerous' here.

Minty **or** her brothers will leave for the north.

The conjunction **or** shows that any one option could happen. Either Minty or her brothers will go to the north, not both.

Minty was down with measles **but** had to keep working.

The conjunction **but** is used to join sentences that show opposite ideas.

There were too many people around, **so** she could only sing a well-known song as a secret message.

The conjunction **so** is used to talk about a result or a decision.

Harriet made many trips to the north **because** she wanted to help the slaves.

The conjunction **because** is used to show a cause or a reason.

B. Complete these sentences with suitable conjunctions.

1. I wore my raincoat __________ it was raining.
2. The dog has hurt its leg, __________ it is walking slowly.
3. She searched the room thoroughly __________ couldn't find the book.
4. Does the cup have coffee __________ tea in it?
5. The train stopped __________ all the passengers got off.
6. It was very hot, __________ Shyam and Azeem went out to play.

Study Skills

Use Your Dictionary

Answer the questions by finding the meanings of the words in bold in your dictionary.

1. What kind of furniture is a **cradle**?
2. What kind of an object is used to **whip** someone?
3. If you stayed in a **cabin**, what kind of a house would it be?
4. If were in an **overcrowded** place, what would it be full of?
5. What kind of transport is a **wagon**?
6. Where would you find the **cellar** in a house?

Listening and Speaking

Imagine that you are a part of a group of people who want to invite Harriet Tubman to honour her work in helping slaves gain freedom. In groups of three, enact a conversation where you meet Harriet and invite her for the event.

Your conversation may include the following steps:

- introducing yourselves to Harriet
- explaining why you want to invite her
- finding out her availability on the suggested date and time
- thanking her for agreeing to attend the event

HC Collaboration and participation

Pen it Down

21ST CENTURY Creativity

Imagine that you are Harriet Tubman. Write a letter to your friend thanking him/her for their help over the years on the Underground Railroad.

You can include the following points in the letter:

- how your friend had helped you
- how you have tried to help others in the same way
- how things are better now compared to the time when you had been helping slaves

Self Assessment

Now I can

- read and understand a biography about a former slave woman who led many slaves to freedom.
- understand idioms, use conjunctions and practise subject-verb agreement.
- use the dictionary to find information about words, enact a conversation inviting someone and write a 'thank you' letter.

Read More

Samuel Morse and the Telegraph: This graphic story by David Seidman talks about how Samuel Morse developed a working telegraph in 1844 that changed the way people communicated.

Overground Railroad: This book by Lesa Cline-Ransome is about a young African-American girl, Ruth Ellen, who travels with her parents on the train to New York, joining the thousands of people escaping the slavery of the American south.

Be Creative!

A. You read the play 'The Girl Who Stepped on the Loaf'. Imagine that it is Christmastime and your class teacher has decided to hold a competition for the best-designed gingerbread house. Gingerbread is a hard, dark-brown cake flavoured with sugar syrup and ginger which is baked in flat sheets and shaped like a house. Write a plan for creating your own gingerbread house using the following points.

Rules for the competition

- It should be made of materials which can be eaten.
- the items used to make the gingerbread house should be given.

Date, time and place for dropping off the gingerbread houses

Prizes for winners

Other information to be provided by the participants

- time taken to make it
- what sets it apart

B. Imagine that you are Harriet Tubman and you are in charge of a train to take slaves to the north. The train is stocked with goods that will give comfort to the slaves. Draw a simple illustration of the train and write about five things that are stocked in it, which will help the escaping slaves. Briefly explain why you think each item will be useful to them.

Literary Genres and Terms

Literary Genres

The stories which you have read in this book are of various types. The following are some common types of stories.

An **adventure** is a type of story or book which has a lot of action, danger, risk and excitement.

A **fable** is a story with a moral lesson at the end. In fables, animals, plants and non-living things often speak like humans.

A **fairy tale** is a story which has magical events and creatures like fairies, elves and goblins.

Light verse is humorous poetry, usually dealing with playful themes and aimed at amusing the reader.

A **descriptive poem** describes in detail the subject of the poem rather than telling a story or talking about feelings.

A **short story** narrates a tale that is only a few pages long.

Non-fiction is a type of prose that is based on real events rather than imaginary ones.

A **folktale** is a story common among people who come from the same background. It is usually passed on in the form of an oral tale.

A **biography** is a book about a famous person and their life events written by another per

A **graphic story** is a story told through words and pictures arranged in a sequence, with dialogues given in speech bubbles.

An **autobiography** is a type of story or book in which the author writes about stories and events from his/her own life.

Literary Terms

Literary terms include common figures of speech. These are the various techniques writers use to convey their message.

A **simile** is a figure of speech in which someone or something is compared to a very different person or thing using 'as' or 'like'. **Example:** He is as brave as a lion.

Personification is a way of imagining non-living things or abstract ideas as human beings with thoughts, actions and emotions. **Example:** The moon danced over the water.

Alliteration is a figure of speech in which the same consonant sound is repeated in consecutive or closely placed words in the same sentence. **Example:** Slithering snakes slither silently through the grass.

Onomatopoeia is the use of words whose pronunciation is similar to the sounds they represent. **Examples:** honk, bang, buzz